MW01626306

TEMPLE RANCH COOKBOOK

A TRADITION OF TEXAS CONSERVATION AND CUISINE

ELLEN TEMPLE AND PATRICK HIEGER

Photographs reproduced with the permission of Chase Fountain and Texas Parks and Wildlife, Austin, Texas; Art Gray Photography, Santa Monica, California; Joe Lowery Photography, Lufkin, Texas; Russell MacMasters Photography, Sonoma, California; David Nix Photography, Dallas, Texas; and Tom Ulrich Photos, West Glacier, Montana

Cover photographs by **Chase Fountain** and **David Nix**.
Ranch photographs: pages 10 and 18 by **Chase Fountain**;
pages iv, 3, 6, 14–15, 17(r), 20 by **Art Gray**; page 9 by **Joe Lowery**;
pages 2 and 15–17(l) by **Russell MacMasters**; and pages 4 and 11–13 by **Tom Ulrich**.
Food photographs by **David Nix**.

Ellen and Buddy Temple would like to extend special thanks to Brandy Savarese, editor, Sheila Parr, art director, and Jessica Pflanz, project manager, of Greenleaf Book Group, who have done such a masterful job of producing this book.

Published and distributed by Emerald Book Company
Austin, Texas
www.emeraldbookcompany.com

Design and composition by Greenleaf Book Group LLC
Cover design by Greenleaf Book Group LLC

Publisher's Cataloging-In-Publication Data
Temple, Ellen.
Temple Ranch cookbook : a tradition of Texas conservation and cuisine / Ellen Temple and Patrick Hieger.—1st ed.
p. : ill. ; cm.
ISBN: 978-1-937110-59-8
1. Cooking—Texas. 2. Cooking, American—Southwestern style.
3. Prairie conservation—Texas. 4. Ranches—Texas—History. 5. Cookbooks.
I. Hieger, Patrick. II. Title.
TX715.2.S69 T46 2013
641.59764 2013946407

Part of the Tree Neutral® program, which offsets the number of trees consumed in the production and printing of this book by taking proactive steps, such as planting trees in direct proportion to the number of trees used: www.treeneutral.com

Printed in China

13 14 15 16 17 18 10 9 8 7 6 5 4 3 2 1

First Edition

TO MY HUSBAND, BUDDY, OUR EL JEFE. YOU ARE THE INSPIRATION AND DRIVING FORCE FOR THE TEMPLE RANCH.

TO OUR CHILDREN: JOHN HURST, WHITNEY TEMPLE, SUSIE TEMPLE AND ROB FEAGIN, HANNAH TEMPLE AND CHRISTOPHER SANDERS.

TO OUR BUCKAROOS: LILLY AND WALTER DUQUETTE, HELEN FEAGIN, MAGGIE GRACE, MARY ELLEN AND ROBERT SANDERS.
—ELLEN

TO MY WIFE, DORIS BRAVO.
—PATRICK

CONTENTS

INTRODUCTION

About two years ago, Patrick Hieger blew in like a norther onto the ranch. Patrick was full of energy and topped off with red hair and beard. He had come to cook for us during the fall and winter seasons, when we entertain many friends and family. Chef Patrick loves to cook, and he also loves to write. In our initial interview, he said that his ultimate goal was to be a food writer. Then he suggested that we might write a cookbook. I let that idea simmer for a year. But when Patrick mentioned it again as a way to celebrate Temple Ranch's twentieth anniversary, Buddy and I decided to do it. This cookbook is the happy result!

One of the wonderful things about this collection of recipes is that Patrick collected them from family, friends, cooks, and chefs who have shared their best meals with us over the years. Patsy and Connie, Sarah and Buddy Z, Clara, Allen, Mary, and Francis all, in some way, contributed to our special dining experiences and to this collection. You'll find one of my recipes too: Chicken and Dumplings; May May's Chicken Spaghetti; Boggy Slough Chili featuring Temple Ranch deer; Lottie's Duck Stew; Sanders' Grilled Quail and Dove; and Hannah and Guthrie's New Year's Lamb Chops and Roasted New Potatoes.

The recipe with the longest history is Boggy Slough Chili. Fifty or so years ago, Gene Shotwell of Lufkin created a simple venison chili recipe with meat, garlic powder, cumin, salt, cayenne, paprika, and chili powder all cooked in suet (beef fat used for frying) in big, black chili pots over gas burners. He served it to Arthur Temple and some other deer hunters, who all loved it. They adopted the recipe for their annual February chili makin', which marks the close of deer season. A battle raged for years between those who were for using suet and those who preferred "sissy" cooking oil. Arch Hollingsworth and John Booker, the Great Chili Makers, perfected the recipe after years of experiments. John reports: "This basic recipe has satisfied a lot of people through the years. From 1968 to 2012, we made 58,201 pounds of chili using basically the same recipe." We share Patrick's version here with a tribute to all who cooked it and enjoyed it all those years!

While we honor our culinary traditions, most of the recipes are Patrick's own. He creatively uses fresh, whole-food ingredients, adding a hint of cumin here or a touch of fresh chili there. He often prepares elegant meals, but he just as often stirs up some

Enjoying company and conversation at the ranch.

down-home cooking like meatloaf or fried chicken with mashed potatoes and gravy—all seasoned and presented with his special touches.

Patrick's most common expression—and our favorite to hear—is "Of course." I'll tell him that we'll have thirty guests for New Year's Eve, including twelve kids and three vegetarians. Then I'll ask, "Can you handle that?" "Of course!" he'll say. He will fix big, hearty meals and then the next week prepare a light "spa" meal. If we can dream it, "of course" Patrick can fix it. Shopping for food for twenty or thirty guests for a week's worth of meals is a challenging task, but Patrick is never discouraged. And he handles small groups seemingly without effort. He's fast, he always prepares plenty of food, and it's consistently delicious and beautifully served.

The Temple Ranch is an extraordinary natural museum of South Texas.

. . .

Our twenty-plus years on the ranch began with the land and its history, the beautiful, hardy plants and the animals that depend on them, and water—or lack of it. The land is our common experience. What fun it is to gather at the Lodge after a day of hunting, riding, walking, or birding and share the harvest from a nearby farm or ranch somewhere in this bountiful country.

– ELLEN TEMPLE

Pitaya, or strawberry cactus, brightens the native landscape at the Temple Ranch.

CONSERVATION

The beloved ranch windmill at sunset.

FROM EL RANCHO LA GLORIA TO TEMPLE RANCH

A TRADITION OF HISTORY, RESTORATION, AND CONSERVATION

Compiled by Brandy Savarese

"WHEN WE SEE LAND AS A COMMUNITY TO WHICH WE BELONG, WE MAY BEGIN TO USE IT WITH LOVE AND RESPECT."
—ALDO LEOPOLD

The Temple Ranch, 11,164 acres of native South Texas chaparral and prairie, tells the story of two families and their commitments to caring for the working landscape of the South Texas Plains. The land that now makes up the Temple Ranch was originally aggregated by Edward Nixon Gray and Rosa Garza Garcia Gray; Rosa herself purchased the first two tracts in 1861. The Gray holding was renowned for its water resources and its ability to support thousands of head of livestock, primarily Merino sheep. Because Gray family success or failure was tied to the landscape, they managed its resources carefully, given their knowledge of range management at the time. The Temple family, who now own and steward the land, have committed themselves to restoring and preserving this large native, rapidly vanishing Texas landscape. From El Rancho la Gloria to Temple Ranch, the landscape is now a model for land conservation in Texas.

EL RANCHO LA GLORIA

Born in 1826 in Auckland, England, Edward Nixon Gray immigrated to Texas as a young boy. At sixteen, Gray began his military service as a seaman aboard the Second Texas Navy's warship *Stephen F. Austin*. He then served in the Texas Mounted Rifles in the Mexican-American War, and in the Texas Home Guard of Duval County during the Civil War. He was referred to as "Captain Gray" until his death, referencing the rank and esteem he had earned in military service.

Captain Gray married Rosa Garza Garcia in 1853, and together they began to build El Rancho la Gloria. They built what became known throughout Duval County as the

The Gray Family assembled at El Rancho la Gloria.

Gray Mansion, a large, two-story home for their family and the site of a school for their twelve children and the children of their ranch hands.

During the late 1800s, El Rancho la Gloria earned notoriety in the area for many reasons, including its forty thousand-acre size, its large herds of livestock, and its production of the softest Merino wool. The Grays are said to have hosted numerous political and social gatherings in their home. The ranch was also the site of another type of South Texas gathering: the Indian raid. The 1873 raid at El Rancho la Gloria is known as the "Last Indian Raid" in popular lore, and it led to the death of the Grays' young son Henry and their shepherd.

Following drought and economic depression in the 1890s, the Grays lost portions of their holdings to foreclosure and termination actions, leaving only the area immediately surrounding the mansion. Captain Gray passed away in 1897, and Rosa sold her remaining two hundred-acre homestead in 1901.

TEMPLE RANCH

The Temple family has worked to preserve and restore the archeological remnants of what once was El Rancho la Gloria while creating a new tradition of land conservation. Their efforts to restore the Duval County property began in 1992, when they purchased ranchland on San Diego Creek. The creek property was wild with brush and bore only remnants of diverse prairie species. Many areas had become overrun with mesquite and prickly pear so thick that the land was nearly impassable, evidence that it had been root-plowed and overgrazed. Buddy Temple's first act of restoration was to knock down some of the overgrowth with a machine the Temples affectionately called the "Green Monster" (a Lawson aerator pulled by a Steiger tractor), in order to give the native grass and forb seed already in the ground a chance to grow. They supplemented these mechanical methods of range management with chemical treatments and carefully orchestrated prescribed fires to encourage the growth of existing native grasses and forbs. Controlling nonnative grasses like buffelgrass and KR bluestem that sprout with the slightest opportunity is an ongoing challenge. The Temples have tried and continue to use just about every method available to restore the diverse prairie ecosystem from pastures historically used for grazing cattle, sheep, and goats.

When the Temples first bought the land, the seed necessary to restore the prairie was not available commercially. But, thanks to the decade-long effort of the Caesar Kleberg Wildlife Research Institute's South Texas Natives project, the Temples can now purchase native grass seeds for the ranch. They have broadcast the native seed from the air and now also use a Truax no-till seed drill built especially for planting the fluffier native seeds. When a pipeline company laid pipe across sixty-six acres of the ranch last year, the Temples decided to replant the cleared

Towering white yucca is one of the ranch's iconic plant species.

Native fauna, like the white-tailed deer, flourish in the ranch's restored landscape.

area, which they call the Pipeline Prairie, with native seed, and they will harvest it in the future as an on-ranch source of the seed needed to support and expand their ongoing ecosystem restoration effort.

As a result of the Temples' efforts and the blessing of rain, the ranch has witnessed the return of native grass species like hooded windmill, blue and Texas gramas, pink pappus, curly mesquite, vine mesquite, multiflowered trichloris, and Arizona cottontop. The benefits of the restoration of the prairie ecosystem are better water absorption, soil retention, and support of the insects, seeds, and ground cover needed for wildlife in South Texas. After winter's rainfall, the springtime blooms with stately white yucca and purple mountain laurel. Blossoming yellow huisache, whitebrush, blackbrush, and coma

Top: The bobwhite quail population has increased thanks to the dedicated efforts of Robert Sanders.

Above: Prickly pear cactus in bloom.

fill the air with their sweet perfumes. Visitors to the ranch delight in the wildflowers that blanket the land, among them yellow bladderpod, huisache daisy, red Indian blanket, pink, purple, and white prickly poppy, blue phlox, and purple vervain. There is nothing more impressive than the fragrances and the colors that rain brings to South Texas.

When the land responds to the rain, so do the birds and animals. Imagine the surprise when a hunter at the ranch spotted a juvenile mountain lion creeping through the brush one February. Lion sightings are rare; it was only the third in twenty years on the ranch. But the ranch is busy with an abundance of white-tailed deer, javelina, badgers, indigo snakes, roadrunners, Harris's hawks, a pair of white-tailed hawks, horned owls, and green jays. The Temples hope that

Top: Huisache daisies blanket the landscape, punctuated by a few white prickly poppies.

Above: The ranch is home to numerous varieties of birds, such as this Vermilion flycatcher.

Pipevine swallowtail butterfly.

Eastern cottontail rabbit.

with habitat restoration and timely rainfall the bobwhite quail population will return to the numbers once enjoyed in the past. Ranch manager Robert Sanders has led the Temple Ranch turkey habitat restoration project, going to such lengths as to build artificial roosts for the birds along the creek bottom. The turkeys have responded well to Sanders's efforts to restore grasses and forbs for their habitat and provide water and supplemental feed sources for their subsistence. He collaborates with Texas A&M University, the National Wild Turkey Federation, and Texas Parks and Wildlife to conduct research at the ranch to identify best practices for managing Rio Grande turkeys.

The plants and wildlife are a source of delight for the Temple family, and they enjoy sharing the experience with others. The ranch is used as a hunting and outdoor recreation retreat for family and friends, and under the direction of events manager Jenny Sanders, it also serves as a site for educational field days for Duval County students, research expeditions, and organized hunts for groups such as the Wounded Warriors and the Texas Brigades. To pay tribute to the family that left an indelible mark on their land, the Temples hosted 150 Gray family descendants and friends in 2009 to celebrate the unveiling of a State of Texas historical marker honoring the legacy of El Rancho la Gloria. New buildings and restored Gray-era structures now dot the ranch landscape, blending the old and the new.

GRAY MANSION AND TEMPLE COTTAGE

The Temples built their Cottage on the site of the Gray Mansion, which had been demolished in 1936. They have preserved remnants of the original building site and have integrated them into the landscaping and architecture of the modern buildings.

The Temple family's efforts to make a home at the ranch for themselves and their guests have been aided by the design and renovation work of Andersson-Wise Architects of Austin. Between 2008 and 2009, the firm designed and constructed the Cottage, the Sunrise Guest House, and the Sunset Guest House to provide modern accommodations for the family and their guests. The ranch's new structures present a rugged exterior of locally made brick punctuated by deep, open porches. According to the architects, the building program was guided by the "importance of making buildings that promote social interaction and quiet contemplation." Following completion of the new buildings, Andersson-Wise undertook the renovation of the Lodge, built in 1974, and the building the Temples affectionately call Big Pop's House, named for Buddy Temple's father. Mimi London, the interior designer for the buildings, has embraced the essence of South Texas and expressed it in the ranch's interiors. The buildings are arranged around a broad courtyard, which features a swimming pool and spa (and a soon-to-be-completed pool cabana designed by Sanders Architecture) that blend with the original features of the site.

The Cottage maximizes the visibility of the site's historic structures: a retaining wall, a rainwater cistern, and the arched-roof cellar, which are in close proximity. In

Above: View across the courtyard pool from the Cottage.

Left: The pool blends seamlessly into the ranch landscape.

order to correct a steep slope in the site, Captain Gray built a retaining wall of *sillares de caliche* (caliche stone blocks) that were a common, locally quarried building material in South Texas. The retaining wall, as well as the cistern and cellar, are constructed of *sillares* mortared with lime and sandy loam mined onsite. The restored wall flanks the Cottage and provides the backdrop for a garden featuring native plants. Catherine O'Connor of Austin was the landscape architect for the rest of the native plants in the compound. Temple Ranch's visible blending of its cultural and natural history—of the old and the new—makes it an extraordinary natural museum of South Texas.

Left: The South Texas-inspired interior of the Lodge game and trophy room.

Above: Looking across the swimming pool toward the Cottage.

THE ROCK HOUSE

Ranch archeologist Jim Warren believes the four-hundred-square-foot Rock House, constructed at approximately the same time as the Gray Mansion, served as a cookhouse and lodging for the Grays' shepherd, who tended the family's large herds of Merino sheep. Local lore and documents filed with the federal government hold it to be the site of the November 1873 Indian raid, during which sixteen-year-old Henry Gray and the shepherd were killed. According to the story, Henry had traveled the few miles between the mansion and the Rock House to deliver provisions to the shepherd. While at the house with a cook, Henry became aware of an approaching band of raiders. Leaving the cook in hiding, Henry tried to reach the shepherd, who was approximately a mile away. When he reached

Top: The Rock House served as a home for the Gray Family's shepherd.

Above: Restored interior of the Rock House.

the shepherd, Henry found him murdered, and he was captured and killed by the raiders. Henry and his father, Edward Nixon Gray, are buried in the family cemetery across the road from ranch headquarters. The Temples began a major reconstruction project on the Rock House in 2007. Jim Warren and his crew shored up the walls and replaced the few crumbled *sillares* with some that they purchased from a rancher who had similar structures on his land. They replaced the missing wooden building components—the door and window frames and roof trusses—with treated yellow pine and the roof with cedar shingles. Following the clue of the original mesquite lintels, they replaced the window shutters and Dutch doors with mesquite lumber harvested from the ranch.

LIME KILN

The Temples and Jim Warren discovered a subterranean lime kiln in a caliche outcrop on the left bank of San Diego Creek, about fifty meters from the Rock House. The Grays constructed it to furnish quick lime for making mortar, plaster, whitewash, and *chipichil* (a mixture of lime, sand, and gravel) flooring for the Rock House and other structures on El Rancho la Gloria constructed of *sillares de caliche*. A lime kiln would have been one of the most important structures in the development of the ranch in the 1800s. Now, an observation deck next to the San Diego Creek pond provides access to the ranch's lime kiln, which is a rare and remarkable archeological discovery.

LABBÉ CHIMNEY AND CEMETERY

The Labbé family cemetery and homestead chimney is the only evidence of the 160 acres settled by the Adolf L. Labbé family in 1864. The cemetery has at least six and as many as thirty gravesites. The earliest recorded interment, based on the extant headstones, was in 1881.

Although their small tract of land used for farming watermelons and cotton was entirely surrounded by El Rancho la Gloria, the family maintained ownership of it until 1965. Nappo Labbé, a descendent of Adolf, still lives in Freer.

. . .

The historic, subterranean root cellar.

The Temples believe strongly in Aldo Leopold's philosophy that "When we see land as a community to which we belong, we may begin to use it with love and respect." For them, the land, water, and wildlife are resources they have been entrusted to steward, and that stewardship includes a responsibility to share with others. Leopold, considered the father of wildlife management, is a touchstone for the family's commitment to Temple Ranch. Fittingly, just one year before its twentieth anniversary, the ranch was awarded the 2011 Leopold Conservation Award for Texas in honor of its transformation from an "overgrazed, overhunted South Texas ranch into a haven for wildlife and a valuable research venue." The ranch has also been recognized by Texas Parks and Wildlife with the 2007 Lone Star Land Steward Award, which recognizes private landowners for excellence in habitat management and wildlife conservation. Although rightfully celebrated, the Temple family needs no more than the good health of their land and wildlife to feel successful in their endeavors. Ellen Temple sums it up neatly: "If we are to continue to live among wild things, ecosystem and habitat restoration must be a major commitment for all in the twenty-first century."

SOURCES

Andersson, Arthur and Chris Wise. "Temple Ranch," in *Natural Houses: The Residential Houses of Andersson-Wise*, 132–52. New York: Princeton Architectural Press, 2010.

Cox, Mike. "Reviving the Ranch: History, Education and Good Land Management Abound at the Leopold Award-Winning Temple Ranch." *Texas Parks and Wildlife Magazine* 69, no.11 November 2011: 41–47.

Sanders, Jenny. *Temple Ranch: A Place of History, Conservation, and Restoration.* Freer, Texas: Temple Ranch, 2011.

Temple, Ellen."My thoughts on restoring habitat. . ." in *Wildlife in Focus VI: Spirit of the Wild* (The Coastal Bend Wildlife Photography Contest), 19. Corpus Christi, Texas: Coastal Bend Wildlife Habitat Education Program, Inc., 2012.

Warren, Jim. *Archeological Investigations and Historical Restoration Efforts on the Temple Ranch in Duval County, Texas*, phase II, vol. 1. Freer Texas: Temple Ranch, 2012.

CUISINE

INTRODUCTION

When I first met Ellen and Buddy Temple, I was at a crossroads in my career. Several years spent climbing the ladder in restaurant kitchens had left my body in pain and my mind in turmoil. Cooking had become a chore much more than a path or a pleasurable experience, and I knew that were I to continue, I would need a renewed enjoyment of the craft. Then I saw an ad on Craigslist calling for chefs to be placed as private chefs with families in various locales. With nothing on my plate and nothing to lose, I sent in my portfolio and hoped for a call. My first assignment was with the Temples, and I cooked for them for two years.

My "agent" had reassured me that my portfolio and résumé were unique, the most creative he had seen, and just the kind of thing his clients were looking for. So as I drove three hours south of Austin into an area of Texas that is more populated by deer than by humans, I decided to go for broke. I served a watermelon salad with mint and a Spanish-style tortilla, which is a style of omelet, for breakfast, and grilled lamb with herb emulsion and olive oil "smashed" potatoes for dinner. I made crepes for dessert, unaware that they are the Temples' absolute favorite. I even made my own ketchup and mayonnaise to serve with lunch, subtle touches that, for Buddy, recalled memories from his childhood of making similar sauces with his mother in their kitchen. Each meal brought new surprises for all of us.

I was worried, though, that my offerings might seem too complex and look like too much work. For some folks, the thought of three handcrafted meals per day might be an overwhelming expectation. I had cooked for people before who told me that they enjoy nothing more than a can of Campbell's tomato soup and that I shouldn't bother trying to improve upon a classic. The Temples were looking for something special, however, something to look forward to at each meal. Their ranch is the fruit of twenty years of labor, and they want to enjoy every minute of it—down to the last dollop of whipped cream on top of warm crepes. I had hit the nail on the head with my simple, handcrafted food that nourished, excited, and kept them wanting more.

After my interview, I knew I wanted to spend time at Temple Ranch. I had never considered the experience of eleven thousand private acres, and I had certainly never imagined being employed at such a marvelous place. But, when I saw the consideration and effort that the Temples had put into remodeling their kitchen (let alone the rest of the "headquarters"), I knew immediately that the ranch would be the place to renew my fervor for cooking, and my spirit. That is to say, just as guests at the ranch have access to idyllic surroundings in which to relax and reinvigorate, the lucky chef is given all the resources necessary to do his best work.

What makes the Temple Ranch so special is its anonymity. If you're not looking for it you'd barely know it's there. The Temples like it that way. Through their own efforts and those of their dedicated employees, the ranch has won prestigious land and conservation awards, garnered mentions for its world-class architecture, and received more than a few compliments from the variety of guests who visit each year. But the praise and awards are not the Temples' motivation for nurturing the property. They are committed to the ranch because they love the land and want to share it with others.

While seclusion and privacy are what give Temple Ranch its overall demeanor and subtle sense of luxury, the buzz of mealtimes gives the ranch its voice. Even before the days of stainless steel appliances and the walk-in cooler, meals at the ranch were prepared by hand, from scratch. Numerous cooks, chefs, and guests themselves have cooked for the Temple family and their visitors throughout the years; each one of them has contributed to what has become a tradition of cuisine at Temple Ranch.

Food is the centerpiece of every visit to the ranch. It's the reason the family gathers in the morning and the hunters come in at midday. Food is how the Temple family's friends and relatives ring in the New Year and celebrate birthdays. For me, food cooked from the heart is the reason I have returned to cooking full time and why my love for food as it's meant to be—a conversation starter and a source of nourishment—has been completely revived.

Since the dining table is the venue at which stories are told and memories shared, why not write a cookbook? Ellen Temple had spent the majority of her career in publishing, and I had blogged about food off and on for some years; it was a natural product of our collaboration. I presented the idea as an opportunity to tell others about the delicious food that has been served at the ranch and to recall the moments and memories that pepper its history of two decades and countless visitors. Each week I received more requests for recipes for certain dishes I had cooked, and I believed that, even though I had spent only a few months at the ranch, the story was worth telling. Now the meals at the Temple Ranch are the inspiration for a book that isn't simply about cooking and recipes; it's also about how a family, the land, and a culture have developed over the last two decades. For me, it is an incredible opportunity not only to be allowed to share my craft with eager guests but also to tell their tales at the same time.

Within these pages I hope you will taste a small part of what I have experienced in my time as chef at the ranch. I also hope you will see a more nuanced portrait of Texas culture than the ten-gallon-hat-wearin', gun-slingin' cowboy trope that so often dominates. Perhaps, too, you'll remember a time when you gathered with friends and family for a meal and conversation. That's what this book is about—coming together.

Rest assured that these recipes are meant to be cooked at home, and not just for trained chefs and special occasions. They are a labor of love and a reminder, for me, of how much I love laboring. For the Temples, I hope this book celebrates their family's twenty years on the ranch, capturing good times outdoors and good meals around the table.

Eat up, enjoy, and keep telling stories.

–PATRICK HIEGER

COOK'S NOTE

The recipes in the *Temple Ranch Cookbook* were adapted from larger-format preparations. Some meals, though, are simply better when cooked in large batches. But don't fret. You will almost certainly have leftovers, and they will most certainly taste even better than the first time the meal was served.

Below, we've included a few explanations that might help you prepare the recipes more easily. Some of the recipes call for specific items that do make each and every one taste better. We hope it goes well for you!

TIPS FOR THE HOME COOK

AGAVE NECTAR. Agave nectar is a sweetener similar to honey but is milder and cooks differently. It is readily available in grocery store baking aisles.

BLENDER. Blenders (including stick or immersion blenders) are appropriate for mixing a loose batter or blending liquids.

BUTTER. When butter is called for in a recipe, it is always unsalted.

DEEP FRYING. With any frying, a deep fryer is ideal because you can set the frying temperature. Home cooks can also use a deep saucepan but are warned to be careful with the hot oil.

FLOUR, ALL-PURPOSE. Unless otherwise specified, all-purpose flour should be used when flour is called for.

FLOUR, WONDRA. Wondra flour is a brand of "instant," low-protein, finely ground flour available in grocery stores.

FRYING OIL. Many recipes at the ranch are deep fried using frying oil. Fryer shortening is recommended, but canola oil can be substituted.

GELATIN, INSTANT. Instant gelatin is widely available in grocery store baking aisles. Knox is the most common brand, but any unflavored, powdered gelatin will work.

MIXER. A stand or hand mixer is typically used for preparing dough. It is important to note that some recipes require the high speed and capacity of a stand mixer.

RONDO. A rondo, also called a brazier, is a wide, shallow pot ideal for simmering, which allows the cooking liquid to enhance flavor and moisture.

SHEET TRAY. A sheet tray or sheet pan is a flat, rectangular metal pan used in the oven. You may also use a cookie or baking sheet.

SILPAT. Silpat is a nonstick silicone mat used for baking on a sheet tray. Parchment coated with nonstick spray is an acceptable substitute.

TAJÍN. Tajín is a brand of lime- and chile-flavored seasoning salt.

APPETIZERS

The great thing about cooking at the Temple Ranch is that there are so many opportunities to connect with and dazzle the guests. From morning to night, every part of a typical day revolves around food, whether it is eggs and fruit salad for breakfast, chicken salad sandwiches for lunch, or a three-course culinary feast for dinner. Guests do come to the ranch to enjoy more than just the food, but whenever mealtime rolls around, there is nary a soul that will hesitate to sit down quickly and await their plate.

As with any great meal, a proper tone must be set from the beginning. Dinners at the ranch always begin with a snack, served about an hour before everyone sits down at the table. These can range from sausage-stuffed jalapeños to bacon-wrapped quail. During hunting season, predinner snacks disappear quickly—the hunters are famished after a long day waiting in deer blinds for the glory of a trophy buck. But they endure the wait, knowing there will be snacks and a great dinner to follow. Other guests, just in for a relaxing weekend and walks throughout the abundant wildflowers, may savor their snacks a little longer. But they, too, anticipate an amazing meal.

When the dinner bell rings and everyone takes a seat, the real show begins. A meal at the ranch is not complete without appetizers, no matter how many snacks were consumed. Dishes like mussels in chorizo-fennel broth or seasonal, roasted Texas vegetables chopped into a salad help guests transition from the day's activities into a more relaxed state. Every meal at Temple Ranch begins with a reminder that your diet will be there waiting for you on Monday, so don't worry. Just sit back, relax, and enjoy your meal.

SANDERS FAMILY STUFFED DOVE POPPERS

15 DOVE, BREASTED AND FULLY DEBONED (OR SUBSTITUTE QUAIL)
½ BOTTLE ALLEGRO GAME TAME, OR YOUR FAVORITE MARINADE
½ BOTTLE ITALIAN DRESSING
1 ONION, COARSELY SLICED
10 JALAPEÑOS, SEEDED AND JULIENNED (THICK FOR HOTTER POPPERS, THIN FOR MILDER POPPERS)
8 OUNCES CREAM CHEESE, DIVIDED INTO 1-TABLESPOON SLICES OR CHUNKS
16 OUNCES THIN BACON, EACH PIECE SLICED IN HALF VERTICALLY

1. Marinate the dove overnight in marinade and dressing.
2. Stuff each breast with a slice of onion, a slice of jalapeño, and a dollop of cream cheese.
3. Wrap each breast with a bacon slice once around. Secure with a skewer or a toothpick that has been soaked in water.
4. Lay dove skewers in a pan and drizzle remaining marinade over them. Allow to come to room temperature before grilling.
5. Grill skewers evenly, until bacon is crisp and jalapeño and onion are a bit soft. Dove should be medium to medium-well and tender (quail should be well-done.)

SMOKED FISH CROSTINI

1 BAGUETTE
2 TABLESPOONS CANOLA OIL
½ POUND SMOKED WHITEFISH
1 CUP MAYONNAISE
¼ CUP CAPERS
ZEST OF 2 LEMONS
1 SHALLOT, MINCED
2 TEASPOONS SALT
MICRO CILANTRO (OR INDIVIDUAL LEAVES OF WHOLE CILANTRO), FOR GARNISH

1. Preheat the oven to 400°F. Slice the baguette into ½-inch-thick slices. Drizzle each slice lightly with canola oil. Bake for 10 minutes, until golden brown. Remove and let cool.
2. In a bowl, break the fish apart into small flakes, taking care to remove any bones.
3. Add the mayonnaise and fold together until a thick paste has formed.
4. Add the capers, lemon zest, shallot, and salt. Mix together until fully incorporated.
5. Place a spoonful of the smoked fish paste on top of each piece of toasted bread. Garnish with micro cilantro. Serve at room temperature.

ROASTED GRAPES AND RICOTTA ON PUMPERNICKEL

1 LOAF PUMPERNICKEL
2 TABLESPOONS CANOLA OIL
2 CUPS SEEDLESS RED GRAPES
¼ CUP OLIVE OIL
2 TEASPOONS SALT
1 TEASPOON BLACK PEPPER
1 CUP WHOLE-MILK RICOTTA CHEESE
2 TABLESPOONS PICKLED MUSTARD SEEDS (SEE RECIPE ON P. 214)
MICRO BASIL, FOR GARNISH

1. Preheat the oven to 400°F. Cut the pumpernickel into 15 even, approximately 2-inch squares (the size of two bites). Drizzle with canola oil. Bake for 15 minutes, until toasted. Remove and let cool.
2. In a bowl, toss the grapes with the olive oil, salt, and pepper. Roast until the grapes have begun to burst and shrivel, approximately 20 minutes. Remove and let cool before serving.
3. Generously layer each piece of toast with a spoonful of ricotta cheese. Top each piece with 2 or 3 grapes. Garnish with mustard seeds and micro basil. Serve at room temperature.

SAUSAGE AND PRETZELS

2 6-OUNCE ITALIAN-STYLE HOT SAUSAGE LINKS, FULLY COOKED
¼ CUP CANOLA OIL
½ ONION, JULIENNED
1 TEASPOON SALT
2 TABLESPOONS YELLOW MUSTARD
16 PRETZEL STICKS

1. Cut each sausage link into 8 individual rounds, approximately ½ inch thick. Set aside.
2. In a sauté pan, warm the canola oil over high heat until it flows freely. Add the onion and salt. Sauté 3 minutes, until the onions become translucent.
3. Add the sausage to the onions. Cook until the individual sausage rounds and the onions have begun to char. Remove from heat.
4. Separate the sausage and the onions. Place several onion strands on each sausage round. Dot each sausage with yellow mustard, then skewer with a pretzel stick. Serve warm.

ALLEN JONAS'S DRAGON FINGERS

Depending on pepper size, the recipe will make 30 to 50 "fingers."

15 TO 20 MEDIUM-SIZE (OR 25 SMALL) JALAPEÑOS
1 POUND OWENS SAUSAGE (REGULAR)
¼ CUP BREAD CRUMBS
¼ CUP FANCY SHREDDED CHEESE
3 TABLESPOONS WORCESTERSHIRE SAUCE (SUBSTITUTE SOY OR TERIYAKI IF NECESSARY)
1 EGG

1. Halve and clean out the jalapeños, discarding seeds.
2. Mix all other ingredients in a bowl.
3. Stuff jalapeño halves with sausage mixture.
4. Grill (or bake in the oven at 350°F) until sausage is done.

HOMEMADE TORTILLA CHIPS WITH QUESO

Tortilla Chips

OIL, FOR FRYING
10 CORN TORTILLAS
TAJÍN (MEXICAN LIME SALT)

1. Using a deep fryer or a deep saucepan, heat one inch of oil to 375°F.
2. Cut each tortilla into quarters. Deep-fry in hot oil until golden and crisp. Remove from fryer and place on a wire rack to strain. Dust with the Tajín immediately, while still hot.
3. Allow tortillas to cool to room temperature. Serve alongside warm queso.

Queso with Beans and Avocado

1 BRICK VELVEETA
1 CUP HEAVY CREAM
2 TEASPOONS SALT
1 CUP BLACK BEANS, COOKED AND STRAINED
1 AVOCADO, DICED
1 TOMATO, DICED

1. Cut the Velveeta into large chunks.
2. In a saucepan, warm the cream, Velveeta, and salt over medium heat, stirring frequently until the cheese has completely melted.
3. Add the beans, avocado, and tomato.
4. Serve warm in a slow cooker with fresh tortilla chips on the side.

Bud Mud (Queso with Sausage and Jalapeño)

I made up this recipe myself, thinking of Mag Mud, a queso at Austin's Magnolia Cafe that has guacamole and black beans in it. This queso is Buddy's absolute favorite, so I named it "Bud Mud."

1 BRICK VELVEETA
1 CUP HEAVY CREAM
1 TEASPOON PLUS 1 TEASPOON SALT
3 TABLESPOONS CANOLA OIL
1 POUND GROUND PORK
1 JALAPEÑO, DICED
2 TEASPOONS BLACK PEPPER
1 TEASPOON CUMIN

1. Cut the Velveeta into large chunks.
2. In a saucepan, warm the cream, Velveeta, and 1 teaspoon salt over medium heat, stirring frequently until the cheese has completely melted.
3. In a sauté pan, warm the canola oil over high heat until it flows freely. Add the ground pork, jalapeño, pepper, cumin, and remaining 1 teaspoon salt. Sauté until the pork is cooked completely through, approximately 10 minutes.
4. Transfer to a slow cooker along with cheese mixture. Serve warm alongside tortilla chips.

FLAUTAS

1 ½ POUNDS CHICKEN THIGHS, BONELESS AND SKINLESS
1 ONION, JULIENNED
1 TABLESPOON PLUS 2 TABLESPOONS SALT
1 TEASPOON PLUS 1 TEASPOON BLACK PEPPER
15 CORN TORTILLAS
1 28-OUNCE CAN PEELED TOMATOES
4 DRIED CHIPOTLE CHILES, TOASTED AND SEEDED
1 BUNCH CILANTRO
¼ CUP LIME JUICE
2 TEASPOONS CUMIN
OIL, FOR FRYING
1 CUP SOUR CREAM, FOR SERVING
2 TOMATOES, CHOPPED, FOR SERVING

1. Preheat the oven to 400°F. Season the chicken and onion with 1 tablespoon salt and 1 teaspoon black pepper. Roast for 20 minutes, until cooked through. Remove and let cool.
2. In the bowl of a food processor, combine the canned tomatoes, chipotle chiles, cilantro, lime juice, cumin, 2 tablespoons salt, and 1 teaspoon black pepper. Puree until smooth.
3. Once the chicken has cooled, chop the thighs into smaller pieces. Combine the chicken and pureed tomato mixture in a saucepan. Bring the mixture to a boil, then reduce to medium-high heat. Cook until the moisture has been cooked out and the mixture is tacky. Remove from heat and let cool.
4. In a deep fryer or a deep saucepan, heat the oil to 375°F. Submerge (or "wet") each tortilla in the hot oil for 10 seconds, then set aside on a tray. (Wetting the tortillas will prevent them from breaking during the assembly process.)
5. Using a fork or tongs, mash and shred the cooled chicken mixture until the chunks are broken up. Fill the center of each tortilla with a large spoonful of chicken, then roll tightly. Skewer the tortillas together in bunches of 3, with a skewer running through either end of the rolled tortillas. This will prevent them from opening during the frying process.
6. Deep-fry each bunch of tortillas in the hot oil until crisp and golden. Remove and top with sour cream and chopped tomatoes. Serve hot.

ARANCINI (FRIED RISOTTO)

¼ CUP CANOLA OIL
2 SHALLOTS, MINCED
1 TABLESPOON SALT
2 CUPS ARBORIO RICE
1 TEASPOON BLACK PEPPER
1 CUP LEMON JUICE
6 CUPS WATER
2 QUARTS OIL, FOR FRYING
1 CUP TOMATO SAUCE, FOR SERVING (SEE RECIPE ON P. 80)

1. In a sauté pan, warm the canola oil over high heat until it flows freely. Add the shallots and salt. Sauté 3 minutes, until translucent. Add the rice and cook 1 minute, until all grains are lightly coated in oil. Add the black pepper. Deglaze with lemon juice.
2. Pour in enough water to just cover the rice. Bring to a boil, then reduce heat to medium high. Cook until the rice has absorbed the water.
3. Repeat the process of adding water and cooking it out, until the risotto is slightly past al dente, approximately 20 minutes. Spread the risotto evenly on a sheet tray. Let cool to room temperature, then refrigerate for 2 hours.
4. Using a deep fryer or a saucepan, heat the frying oil to 375°F. Using both hands, roll and compress the chilled risotto into tightly packed balls, each roughly the size of a golf ball.
5. Fry in oil until golden brown. Remove and place on a wire rack. Serve warm with tomato sauce on the side.

PIGS IN A BLANKET WITH BARBECUE SAUCE

1 CUP APPLE CIDER VINEGAR
½ CUP DIJON MUSTARD
1 CUP ROOT BEER
½ CUP BROWN SUGAR
1 TABLESPOON SALT
2 TEASPOONS BLACK PEPPER
FLOUR, FOR ROLLING DOUGH
1 PACKAGE FROZEN PUFF PASTRY SHEETS, THAWED
1 PACKAGE COCKTAIL WIENERS
½ CUP BUTTER, MELTED

1. In a saucepan, bring the vinegar, mustard, root beer, brown sugar, salt, and pepper to a boil. Reduce heat to medium, then cook until mixture is reduced by half. Remove from heat and set aside.
2. Preheat the oven to 400°F. Unfold the thawed puff pastry sheets onto a lightly floured surface. Using a rolling pin, gently roll the sheets out to a ¼-inch-thick layer. With a pizza wheel, cut the puff pastry into 4 × 1-inch strips. Wrap each miniature wiener in a strip of puff pastry and place the wrapped wieners on a sheet tray. Brush each with the melted butter.
3. Bake for 10 minutes, until golden brown. Remove and serve warm with the barbecue sauce.

STEAMED MUSSELS IN CHORIZO-FENNEL BROTH

Mussels have a "beard," threads that stick out from the seam, by which they attach to a rope or other support in the sea. Typically, store-bought mussels will be precleaned, but it's a good policy to give them a once-over and remove the beard. Mussels should also always be closed. If they are not, they are bad and should be discarded.

1 BULB FENNEL, WITH FRONDS
8 OUNCES DRIED SPANISH-STYLE CHORIZO
¼ CUP CANOLA OIL
1 TABLESPOON SALT
2 TEASPOONS BLACK PEPPER
2 POUNDS FRESH MUSSELS, RINSED AND CLEANED
1 BOTTLE (12 OUNCES) MEXICAN BEER
½ CUP BUTTER
1 BUNCH PARSLEY, CHOPPED, FOR GARNISH
1 BAGUETTE, SLICED

1. Cut the tops off the fennel. Remove fronds from the tops and set aside. Cut the fennel bulb in half. Remove the core from each half, then julienne each half. Cut the remaining tops into rounds and set aside.
2. Cut the chorizo links in half, lengthwise, then cut into ¼-inch-thick slices.
3. In a saucepan with a lid, warm the canola oil over high heat until it flows freely. Add the julienned fennel, chorizo, salt, and pepper. Cover and cook for 5 minutes, until the fennel has softened.
4. Add the mussels and cook 1 minute, stirring constantly. Pour in the beer, then cover. Cook over high heat until all the mussels have opened, approximately 3 minutes. Remove the cover and add the butter.
5. Once the butter has melted, pour the contents of the saucepan into a large bowl or divide evenly among small bowls. Garnish with the chopped parsley. Serve hot with baguette.

GAZPACHO

12 ROMA TOMATOES
2 LOAVES FRENCH BREAD, TORN IN PIECES (4 CUPS)
1 BUNCH PARSLEY
½ CUP SHERRY VINEGAR
7 TEASPOONS SALT
2 TEASPOONS BLACK PEPPER
1 TEASPOON SPANISH PAPRIKA
2 CUPS WATER

1. In the bowl of a food processor, combine the tomatoes, bread, parsley, sherry vinegar, salt, pepper, and paprika. Puree until the tomatoes have liquefied and the bread is incorporated.
2. Slowly pour in the water until a smooth, thick texture has been reached. The soup should not be runny or overly watery. Serve chilled.

GREEN SALAD

8 CUPS SPRING MIX, LOOSELY PACKED
3 TEASPOONS SALT
1 ½ TEASPOONS BLACK PEPPER
1 CUP CIDER-VANILLA VINAIGRETTE (SEE RECIPE ON P. 215)
½ CUP BREAD CRUMBS (SEE RECIPE ON P. 217)

1. Place the greens in a large mixing bowl. Season the leaves with the salt and pepper, taking care to spread the spices evenly across the leaves.
2. Pour the dressing in a ring around the edge of the bowl, then spiral toward the center. Using both hands, gently toss until all the leaves are coated and have a slight sheen.
3. Place the dressed greens in a presentation bowl and top with the bread crumbs. Serve immediately.

ICEBERG WEDGE WITH RANCH DRESSING

1 HEAD ICEBERG LETTUCE
1 LARGE TOMATO
6 STRIPS APPLEWOOD-SMOKED BACON, COOKED UNTIL CRISP
2 CUPS RANCH DRESSING (SEE RECIPE ON P. 217)
CRACKED BLACK PEPPER, FOR GARNISH

1. Remove the core from the head of lettuce. Remove any brown outer leaves. Cut lettuce head in half vertically. Cut each half into three even wedges.
2. Cut the tomato in half, then cut each half into three even wedges. Set aside.
3. Chop the crisp bacon into small bits. Set aside.
4. Place one wedge of lettuce on a plate. Using a small ladle or a measuring cup, liberally pour ⅓ cup of dressing over each wedge of lettuce and onto the plate. Place a wedge of tomato in the dressing on the plate. Sprinkle with bacon bits and garnish with pepper. Serve cold.

LUNCH

I have come to the firm conclusion that in order to understand luxury, one must simply have the time to sit down and enjoy a midday meal on a daily basis. Whether it is a turkey sandwich, a hearty bowl of chili with cornbread, or a made-from-scratch plate of chef-prepared food, it really doesn't matter. Time is the biggest factor that distinguishes good lunches from great ones. A light breeze and a good view make the great ones even better. Luckily for guests at Temple Ranch, time is in abundance and the views are inescapable.

For restaurant chefs, lunch can be burdensome. Folks on their lunch break never feel like they have time to relax. In South Texas, though, where a gentle breeze is rarely in short supply, the dishes are bound to become new lunch favorites, and guests have very little to worry about other than finding a place to sit.

The dishes in this section are a blend of meals designed to warm and revive hunters, after long mornings of hunting, and guests in search of a more leisurely visit to the ranch. It is food designed to extend the feeling that comes with long walks through patches of wildflowers and clusters of butterflies. For the hunters, hot sandwiches and hearty soups are always in high demand. For couples' weekends and those later in the season when the weather begins to warm up again, abundant salads and pan-fried fish become the standard. There's plenty in between, too, like made-from-scratch veggie burgers and Mary Cadena's enchiladas. Even with the promise of a big, taste-bud thrilling dinner each night, lunch is never an afterthought. It gives family and guests the energy for horseback riding and trips out to the shooting shed. Children hurry through their plates in anticipation of the day's first dessert. And time, the most important ingredient to any successful lunch at Temple Ranch, languidly lazes on, urging guests to do only what suits them and nothing more.

LODGE

ALLEN JONAS'S PAN SAUSAGE AND CABBAGE

16 OUNCES KIELBASA SAUSAGE, CUT INTO 1-INCH PIECES
1 MEDIUM ONION, THINLY SLICED
1 GREEN BELL PEPPER, JULIENNED
6 CUPS CABBAGE, COARSELY CHOPPED
1 CUP BEER (OR DRY WHITE WINE OR CHICKEN BROTH)
½ TEASPOON CARAWAY SEEDS
½ TEASPOON SALT
½ TEASPOON BLACK PEPPER

1. Sauté sausage in a large, heavy skillet over medium heat until browned. Drain on paper towels.
2. Add onion and bell pepper to skillet and sauté 2 to 3 minutes.
3. Add cabbage and cook 8 minutes, stirring often.
4. Add sausage, beer (or wine or broth), caraway seeds, salt, and pepper. Reduce heat to medium low and cook 10 minutes or until cabbage is tender.
5. Serve immediately.

ACAPULCO SANDWICHES

6 SLICES WHOLE WHEAT BREAD
6 THICK SLICES BLACK FOREST HAM
6 SLICES SWISS CHEESE
12 SLICES TOMATO
1 RED ONION, SLICED INTO RINGS
1 AVOCADO, SLICED

1. Preheat the oven to 400°F. Place the bread on a sheet tray and warm until lightly toasted, approximately 6 minutes. Remove from the oven.
2. Top each piece of toasted bread with one slice of ham. Top the ham with the cheese. Place two slices of tomato and several onion rings on top of the cheese. Return the sandwiches to the oven and let cook until the cheese has melted, approximately 5 minutes.
3. Remove the warm sandwiches from the oven and top with sliced avocado. Serve warm and open-faced.

ELLEN TEMPLE'S CHICKEN AND DUMPLINGS

8 CHICKEN BREASTS, BONELESS AND SKINLESS
2 ONIONS, CHOPPED
4 CARROTS, CHOPPED
4 STALKS CELERY, CHOPPED
6 QUARTS WATER
1 CUP BUTTER
2 ½ CUPS FLOUR (APPROXIMATE)
1 TABLESPOON BAKING POWDER
2 TABLESPOONS SALT
1 TABLESPOON BLACK PEPPER

1. In a large pot, combine the chicken breasts, chopped vegetables, and water. Bring to a boil, then reduce to a simmer. Let cook 1 hour.
2. Strain the broth into a container and set aside. Remove the cooked chicken from the vegetables and let cool. Discard the vegetables.
3. Combine flour, salt, and pepper.
4. In a bowl, combine ½ cup of the hot broth and the butter. Stir in the flour mixture bit by bit, until a slightly tacky but firm dough is formed (this may require more or less than 2 ½ cups of flour). Roll out the dough on a floured surface until it is flat, approximately ¼ inch thick. Cut the dough into 1-½-inch squares.
5. Pour the rest of the strained broth into a broad, shallow pot and bring just to a boil over medium-high heat. Add the dough pieces and let simmer 20 minutes. The broth will start to thicken as the dumplings cook.
6. Shred the chicken by hand and return it to the thickened broth and dumplings. Let simmer until the chicken is warmed through. Serve hot immediately.

ROBALO-STYLE SNAPPER

1 CUP FLOUR
1 TABLESPOON SALT
1 TEASPOON BLACK PEPPER
¾ CUP CANOLA OIL
4 SNAPPER FILETS, SKINLESS
1 HEAD ICEBERG LETTUCE, SHREDDED
4 RADISHES, SLICED
¼ CUP OLIVE OIL
¼ CUP LIME JUICE
1 TEASPOON SALT

1. In a Pyrex or other long glass dish, mix the flour, salt, and pepper until fully incorporated. Dredge each snapper filet on both sides until fully covered.
2. In a cast iron pan, warm the canola oil over high heat until it flows freely. Place the dredged filets in the hot oil, two at a time. Cook on each side approximately 3 minutes, or until the filets turn a deep, golden brown. Remove the cooked filets and let drain on a wire rack or a paper towel.
3. In a mixing bowl, combine the lettuce, radishes, olive oil, lime juice, and salt. Mix together until all ingredients are covered in lime juice and olive oil.
4. Serve each snapper filet on a plate with a mound of salad to the side.

CHICKEN SALAD

6 CHICKEN BREASTS, BONELESS AND SKINLESS
¼ CUP CANOLA OIL
1 TABLESPOON SALT
2 TEASPOONS BLACK PEPPER
1 CUP TEMPLE FAMILY MAYONNAISE (SEE RECIPE ON P. 216)
1 RED ONION, FINELY DICED
2 CUPS SEEDLESS RED GRAPES, CUT IN HALF
1 ½ CUPS TEXAS PECANS, CHOPPED AND TOASTED
1 TABLESPOON LEMON JUICE
1 TABLESPOON PAPRIKA

1. Preheat the oven to 375°F. In a bowl, season the chicken breasts with the canola oil, salt, and pepper. Roast for 20 minutes or until cooked through. Remove from oven and let cool.
2. In a bowl, mix together the mayonnaise, red onion, grapes, pecans, lemon juice, and paprika.
3. Dice cooled chicken into ½-inch chunks and add to bowl.
4. Serve as desired (with lettuce and toast points, in finger sandwiches, on flatbread, with toasted focaccia, etc.)

MARY CADENA'S CHALUPAS

OIL, FOR FRYING
4 CORN TORTILLAS
2 CUPS BLACK BEANS, COOKED AND STRAINED
½ CUP PLUS 4 TABLESPOONS CANOLA OIL
1 ONION, DICED
1 JALAPEÑO, DICED
1 TOMATO, DICED
2 CHICKEN BREASTS, GRILLED AND SHREDDED
1 TABLESPOON SALT
1 TEASPOON BLACK PEPPER
1 CUP QUESO FRESCO, CRUMBLED
1 CUP MOZZARELLA, SHREDDED
2 CUPS ICEBERG LETTUCE, SHREDDED
JUICE OF 1 LIME

1. Deep-fry the whole tortillas until crisp. Set aside on a wire rack.
2. Using a food processor, puree the black beans with the ½ cup canola oil until smooth.
3. In a saucepan, warm the bean mixture over low heat, and hold.
4. In a sauté pan, warm the 4 tablespoons canola oil over high heat until it flows freely. Sauté the onion for 1 minute or until translucent. Add the jalapeño, tomato, chicken, salt, and pepper. Cook until the chicken is warm.
5. Spread the warm black beans on each tortilla, forming a thick layer. Sprinkle the queso fresco over the beans, then top with the chicken and vegetable mixture. Cover with the mozzarella.
6. Top each chalupa with lettuce. Drizzle with lime juice. Serve warm.

"KING RANCH" CHICKEN CASSEROLE

6 CHICKEN BREASTS, BONELESS AND SKINLESS
1 TABLESPOON PLUS 1 TEASPOON SALT
1 TEASPOON BLACK PEPPER
2 TABLESPOONS PLUS ¼ CUP CANOLA OIL
2 BELL PEPPERS, JULIENNED
1 ONION, JULIENNED
2 CUPS MUSHROOMS, SLICED
2 TABLESPOONS CUMIN
½ CUP BUTTER
4 CUPS HEAVY CREAM
18 TORTILLAS, CUT INTO QUARTERS
4 ½ CUPS AMERICAN CHEESE, SHREDDED

1. Preheat the oven to 400°F. Season the chicken breasts with 1 tablespoon salt, pepper, and 2 tablespoons canola oil. Roast on a sheet tray for approximately 20 minutes or until cooked through. Let cool, then dice.
2. In a large sauté pan, warm the ¼ cup canola oil over medium-high heat until it flows freely. Add the bell peppers, onion, and 1 teaspoon salt. Sauté 3 minutes. Add the mushrooms, diced chicken, cumin, and butter. Cook until the butter has melted.
3. Pour the cream over the chicken and vegetables. Reduce heat to medium. Cook, stirring frequently, until the cream has thickened and reduced by half (approximately 20 minutes). Do not allow the cream to hit a hard boil, or it will separate. Once thickened, remove from heat and set aside.
4. Spray a 9 × 13-inch baking dish with nonstick spray. Layer the bottom with quartered tortillas, approximately 18 quarters per layer. Spread about one-quarter of the chicken mix over the tortillas. Cover with about one-quarter of the cheese.
5. Repeat step 4 to the top of the dish, ensuring that each tortilla layer is covered by thick layers of chicken and cheese. Bake at 400°F for 20 minutes, or until the cheese is melted and bubbly.

MARY CADENA'S ENCHILADAS

These enchiladas are best made ahead of time and allowed to cool. Once the sauce has cooled and set, allowing the flavors to meld, the enchiladas can be reheated and served.

Enchiladas

2 POUNDS CHICKEN THIGHS, BONELESS AND SKINLESS
1 TABLESPOON SALT
1 TEASPOON BLACK PEPPER
¼ CUP PLUS 2 CUPS CANOLA OIL
1 TABLESPOON CHILI POWDER
1 ONION, JULIENNED
1 BELL PEPPER, JULIENNED
1 JALAPEÑO, SEEDED AND DICED
30 CORN TORTILLAS
4 CUPS AMERICAN CHEESE, SHREDDED

1. Preheat the oven to 400°F. Season the chicken thighs with the salt, pepper, ¼ cup canola oil, and chili powder. Toss with the onion, bell pepper, and jalapeño. Roast on a sheet tray for 20 minutes or until chicken is cooked through.
2. Remove from oven and allow to cool. Reduce oven temperature to 375°F. Chop the chicken and reserve with the roasted vegetables.
3. In a large sauté pan, warm the 2 cups of canola oil over medium heat. "Wet" each tortilla in the warm oil for 10 seconds. (Wetting the tortillas will help prevent them from breaking during the assembly process.)
4. Divide the chicken mixture evenly among the tortillas. Roll each filled tortilla into a tube. Place the filled tortillas in a 9 × 15-inch oven-safe dish, seams down and tightly packed. Cover with the cheese, and top generously with Enchilada Sauce (recipe follows). Tap the pan so the sauce flows between the tortillas.
5. Bake for 15 minutes, or until the cheese is melted and bubbly. If reserving for the next day, refrigerate overnight and then cook at 375°F for 35 minutes, or until a knife inserted comes out hot.

Enchilada Sauce

¾ CUP CANOLA OIL
1 CUP FLOUR
6 CUPS WATER
3 TABLESPOONS CHILI POWDER
1 TABLESPOON SALT
BLACK PEPPER TO TASTE

1. In a saucepan, warm the canola oil over medium-high heat until it flows freely. Add the flour. Cook, stirring frequently, until the mixture forms a sandy paste (approximately 5 minutes).
2. Add the water, chili powder, salt, and pepper. Cook until the sauce has thickened to a gravy-like consistency.

MARY CADENA'S FLOUR TORTILLAS

4 CUPS FLOUR
2 TEASPOONS BAKING POWDER
2 TEASPOONS SALT
¾ CUP VEGETABLE SHORTENING
1 ½ CUPS BOILING WATER

1. In a bowl, mix together the dry ingredients. Using your hands, fold in the shortening until the mixture reaches a loose, grainy texture.
2. Pour in the water and mix until a smooth, pliable ball of dough is formed. Knead 1 minute.
3. Portion the dough into 2-ounce balls. Form each ball into a small disc, then use a rolling pin to roll each portion into a tortilla approximately 6 inches in diameter.
4. On a hot, dry griddle pan, cook each tortilla until the side facing up begins to bubble. Flip and cook 1 more minute.

PIZZA

The first time I served pizza at Temple Ranch, I was not sure how it would be received. Once it was ready, I yelled, "Pizza party!" I have never seen grown men run to a table so fast. Needless to say, pizza has been a lunch staple ever since.

Tomato Sauce

1 26-OUNCE CAN WHOLE PEELED TOMATOES
1 BUNCH PARSLEY, CHOPPED
1 BUNCH BASIL, CHOPPED
3 TABLESPOONS CANOLA OIL
1 ONION, JULIENNED
2 TABLESPOONS SALT
2 TEASPOONS PEPPER
½ CUP PLUS ½ CUP WATER
1 6-OUNCE CAN TOMATO PASTE
½ CUP LEMON JUICE

1. In a food processor or blender, puree the peeled tomatoes and herbs until smooth. Set aside.
2. In a saucepan, warm the canola oil over medium-high heat until it flows smoothly around the pan. Add the onions, salt, and pepper. Cook over high heat until the onions begin to char the bottom of the pan. Deglaze with ½ cup of water. Repeat this process of charring and deglazing with the other ½ cup of water.
3. Add the tomato paste and sauté until it begins to stick. Deglaze with the lemon juice.
4. Add the pureed tomatoes. Cook until just boiling.
5. Remove sauce from the heat. Puree in a blender until smooth. Set aside and let cool.

Pizza Dough

Preparation requires a stand mixer due to the super-firm dough.

4 CUPS PLUS ½ CUP FLOUR (APPROXIMATE)
2-¼-OUNCE ENVELOPE ACTIVE DRY YEAST (4 ½ TEASPOONS)
2 CUPS WARM WATER (APPROXIMATELY 110°F TO 120°F)
2 TABLESPOONS SALT
1 TABLESPOON BLACK PEPPER
4 TABLESPOONS OLIVE OIL
FLOUR FOR KNEADING

1. In the bowl of a stand mixer, combine the 4 cups flour, yeast, water, salt, pepper, and olive oil. Using the mixer's dough hook attachment, mix the ingredients until a moist, slightly sticky dough has formed. If necessary, use the remaining ½ cup of flour to soak up excess moisture until the dough is stretchy and only lightly sticky to the touch.
2. Remove all dough from the bowl and place on a lightly floured surface. Allow the dough to pick up enough flour so it is lightly dusted. With hands on the bottom, fold the dough into itself until a smooth ball has formed.
3. Place the dough in a lightly greased container and cover loosely with plastic. Let the dough rise (or "proof") until it has doubled or tripled in size. Proofing should take place in a warm (90°F to 100°F) environment.
4. Once the dough has risen, remove it from the container and place it on a lightly floured surface. Cut into three equal portions.

Assembly

PIZZA DOUGH
2 CUPS CORNMEAL (APPROXIMATE)
12 OUNCES TOMATO SAUCE (APPROXIMATE)
6 CUPS SHREDDED CHEESE (APPROXIMATE)
VARIOUS VEGETABLES AND MEATS

1. Preheat the oven to 450°F. Lightly dust three pizza pans with cornmeal. Using a lightly floured rolling pin, roll out each dough ball to fit the shape of the pizza pan. Place the dough on the pans.
2. Ladle a layer of sauce (approximately 4 ounces) onto each pizza, leaving a desired amount of crust. Cover sauce with the cheese. Dress each pizza with various toppings.
3. Bake pizzas for 15 minutes or until crust is golden brown. Remove and slice with a pizza wheel. Serve hot.

CHICKEN FAJITAS WITH ACAPULCO RICE AND PINTO BEANS

Chicken Fajitas

3 POUNDS CHICKEN THIGHS, BONELESS AND SKINLESS
1 TEASPOON CHILI POWDER
1 TEASPOON TAJÍN (MEXICAN LIME SALT)
2 TEASPOONS SALT
1 TEASPOON BLACK PEPPER
1 TEASPOON CUMIN
1 TEASPOON PAPRIKA
½ CUP PLUS ¼ CUP CANOLA OIL
1 RED BELL PEPPER, DICED
1 ONION, DICED
MARY CADENA'S FLOUR TORTILLAS (SEE RECIPE ON P. 79)

1. Preheat the oven to 400°F. In a bowl, combine the chicken, spices, and ½ cup canola oil. Roast until cooked through, approximately 20 minutes. Let cool in the pan juices.
2. Once cool, chop the cooked pieces into smaller strips, making sure to reserve the pan juices.
3. In a sauté pan, warm ¼ cup canola oil over high heat until it flows freely. Add the bell pepper and onion. Sauté 3 minutes or until translucent. Add the chicken and reserved juices. Serve hot with Mary Cadena's Flour Tortillas, alongside Acapulco Rice and Mary Cadena's Pinto Beans (recipes follow).

Acapulco Rice

This recipe attempts to recreate the Temples' favorite Mexican rice.

2 TABLESPOONS CANOLA OIL
1 ONION, DICED
2 TABLESPOONS SALT
1 TEASPOON BLACK PEPPER
¼ CUP LIME JUICE
2 CUPS LONG-GRAIN WHITE RICE
½ CUP BUTTER
3 ½ CUPS WATER

1. In a saucepan, heat the canola oil until it flows freely. Add the onions and sauté for 2 minutes or until translucent. Add the salt, pepper, and lime juice. Sauté for 1 minute.
2. Add the rice and sauté until all grains have been lightly glazed with oil, approximately 1 minute.
3. Add the butter and water. Bring the rice to a boil and cook until only a thin layer of water remains on top of the grains, stirring occasionally. Cover and reduce heat to low.
4. Cook for 8 minutes. Immediately remove from heat and let stand 5 minutes, covered. Remove rice from the pot and fluff. Serve hot.

Mary Cadena's Pinto Beans

8 CUPS PINTO BEANS
5 QUARTS WATER
3 TABLESPOONS SALT

1. Rinse the beans thoroughly prior to cooking, to ensure that all dirt and small stones have been removed.
2. In a large pot, combine the rinsed beans, water, and salt. Allow the beans to come to a boil over medium heat, then reduce the heat slightly. Cook 2 hours or until the beans are tender.
3. Serve in a bowl, family style, alongside Chicken Fajitas or Mary Cadena's Enchiladas (see recipe on p. 76), Allen Jonas's Carne Guisada (see recipe on p. 117), etc.

CHICKEN BISCUIT POT PIE

Biscuits

See Biscuits recipe on p. 196. Follow directions through step 5, cutting biscuits with a larger mold to more closely fit the pot pie dish. Set biscuits aside, uncooked.

Chicken Pot Pie

1 CUP BUTTER
1 CUP FLOUR
3 TABLESPOONS SALT
1 TABLESPOON BLACK PEPPER
1 TABLESPOON SAGE
2 CARROTS, CHOPPED
1 ONION, CHOPPED
4 STALKS CELERY, CHOPPED
1 QUART CHICKEN STOCK, UNSALTED
4 CHICKEN BREASTS, FULLY COOKED AND DICED

1. Preheat the oven to 425°F.
2. In a large saucepan, melt the butter over high heat. Once melted, stir in the flour to form a roux. Stir frequently until the mixture turns light brown and smells nutty, approximately 5 minutes. Add the spices and vegetables. Cook 2 minutes.
3. Pour in the chicken stock and whisk together until all ingredients are blended. Cook until mixture reaches a loose, gravy-like consistency, approximately 5 minutes.
4. Add the chicken. Cook to the consistency of a thick gravy, approximately 10 minutes.
5. Evenly divide the mixture into oven-safe bowls (cereal or similar size). Place a biscuit on top of each bowl.
6. Bake for 20 minutes or until the biscuit is golden brown. Remove and serve immediately.

FRANCIS FAUQUENOT VENISON CHILI WITH JALAPEÑO CORNBREAD

This recipe will serve a large party.

Venison Chili

3 ⅓ POUNDS VENISON, DICED
2 TABLESPOONS PAPRIKA
2 TABLESPOONS CUMIN
1 TABLESPOON CAYENNE PEPPER
3 TABLESPOONS CHILI POWDER
SALT AND BLACK PEPPER, TO TASTE
2 MEDIUM ONIONS, FINELY DICED
3 CLOVES GARLIC, MINCED
2 GREEN PEPPERS, DICED
1 ⅓ POUNDS RED BEANS
¼ CUP OLIVE OIL
1 14-OUNCE CAN OF TOMATOES, DICED
4 TEASPOONS TOMATO PASTE
1 SPRIG THYME
1 SPRIG PARSLEY
2 BAY LEAVES
SOUR CREAM, FOR GARNISH
1 BUNCH CILANTRO, CHOPPED, FOR GARNISH
SHREDDED GRUYÈRE OR CHEDDAR, FOR GARNISH

1. Soak beans for at least 2 hours. Drain. Cover with water and boil for 20 minutes. Drain. Set aside.
2. In a sauté pan, warm olive oil over high heat and sauté the venison. Do not overcrowd the pan—work in small batches if necessary. Season with spices, salt, and pepper. Remove from heat and set aside.
3. In a large skillet or Dutch oven, sweat the onion, garlic, and green peppers without coloration for approximately 15 minutes.

4. Add the olive oil and venison to the Dutch oven, along with the diced tomatoes, tomato paste, thyme, parsley, and bay leaves. Cook on medium heat for approximately 2 ½ hours, adding water if needed.
5. Garnish each serving with sour cream, cilantro, and cheese. Serve with Jalapeño Cornbread (recipe follows).

Jalapeño Cornbread

2 CUPS COARSE CORNMEAL
2 CUPS FLOUR
2 TABLESPOONS SALT
4 EGGS
1 CUP CANOLA OIL
8 TEASPOONS BAKING POWDER
4 TABLESPOONS SUGAR
1 TABLESPOON BLACK PEPPER
2 CUPS MILK
1 JALAPEÑO, DICED
1 EAR YELLOW CORN, KERNELS CUT FROM THE COB

1. Preheat the oven to 400°F.
2. Combine all ingredients in the bowl of a stand mixer. Beat together until fully incorporated into a wet mix.
3. Pour ingredients into a greased 9 × 13-inch pan. Bake 30 minutes or until golden on top. Remove and let cool 30 minutes. Serve with Venison Chili.

BOGGY SLOUGH CHILI

The Boggy Slough Hunting Club has made more than 50,000 pounds of this chili in the last fifty years. That's quite a pedigree! The club makes it in much larger batches, but this smaller recipe will work just fine for folks at home.

1 CUP CANOLA OIL
2 POUNDS VENISON, DICED INTO ½-INCH CUBES
1 TABLESPOON CHILI POWDER
2 TEASPOONS CUMIN
1 TEASPOON GARLIC POWDER
1 TEASPOON PAPRIKA
1 TEASPOON SALT
1 CLOVE GARLIC, CHOPPED
1 8-OUNCE CAN TOMATO PASTE
WATER
FRITOS, FOR GARNISH
DICED ONIONS, FOR GARNISH
SHREDDED CHEDDAR OR AMERICAN CHEESE, FOR GARNISH

1. In a broad, 10-quart pot or rondo, warm the canola oil over medium-high heat until it flows freely. Once the oil is hot, add the diced venison. Cook until meat has been browned on all sides.
2. Add the spices and garlic to the browned meat. Cook 2 minutes, until the aroma of the spices is strong. Add the tomato paste and cook 1 minute.
3. Pour enough water into the pot to cover the meat and to achieve desired consistency. (For a thicker chili, add only enough water so the meat doesn't burn. For a thinner consistency, add more water during the cooking process.) Let the liquid come to a boil, then reduce to a simmer over medium heat. Cook until the meat is tender, approximately 2 to 3 hours.
4. Garnish each serving with Fritos, onions, and cheese. Serve hot.

GREEN POZOLE (HOMINY STEW)

3 POUNDS TOMATILLOS, CHOPPED
4 JALAPEÑOS, SEEDED AND CHOPPED
1 BUNCH CILANTRO, CHOPPED
2 QUARTS WATER
1 CUP LIME JUICE
2 15-½-OUNCE CANS WHITE HOMINY, STRAINED
6 TABLESPOONS SALT
1 TABLESPOON BLACK PEPPER
2 POUNDS PORK, ROASTED AND SHREDDED
1 CUP CABBAGE, SHREDDED, FOR GARNISH
1 CUP QUESO FRESCO, CRUMBLED, FOR GARNISH

1. Combine the tomatillos, jalapeños, cilantro, water, and lime juice in a 6- or 8-quart saucepan. Bring to a boil and simmer for 30 minutes. Remove from heat. Puree in a blender until smooth.
2. Return the pureed liquid to the pot. Add the hominy, salt, and pepper. Simmer over medium heat for 30 minutes or until the broth has thickened slightly. Add the pork and cook over medium heat for 10 minutes.
3. Garnish each serving with cabbage and queso fresco. Serve hot.

HAMBURGERS AND SMOKED HOME FRIES

Smoked Home Fries

4 LARGE RUSSET POTATOES
3 TABLESPOONS SALT
1 TABLESPOON BLACK PEPPER
½ CUP OLIVE OIL
1 CUP CORNMEAL

1. Preheat the oven to 400°F.
2. Cut each potato into wedges, approximately 6 to 8 pieces per potato. Toss with salt, pepper, and olive oil until thoroughly coated. Add the cornmeal and toss until all the potatoes are lightly dusted.
3. Roast the potatoes on a sheet tray until tender, approximately 25 minutes. Remove and let cool to room temperature.
4. Place the potatoes in a smaller, perforated pan. When cooking the burgers, place the pan of potatoes on a separate part of the grill to pick up smoke. Serve hot alongside Hamburgers (recipe follows).

Hamburgers

2 POUNDS 85% LEAN GRASS-FED GROUND BEEF
2 TABLESPOONS SALT
1 TABLESPOON BLACK PEPPER
4 HAMBURGER BUNS
1 TOMATO, SLICED
ROMAINE LETTUCE
SLICED VERMONT CHEDDAR (OPTIONAL)
KETCHUP AND MUSTARD (OPTIONAL)

1. Thoroughly combine the ground beef, salt, and pepper. Portion the meat into 4 equal-sized patties. Grill to desired doneness.
2. While grilling the burgers, place the buns on a cooler portion of the grill to toast and pick up smoke. Remove once buns have browned.
3. Place one burger on each bun and dress with tomato, lettuce, cheese, ketchup, and mustard. Serve hot.

VEGGIE BURGERS WITH BLACK-EYED PEA HUMMUS

Black-Eyed Pea Hummus

2 CUPS DRIED BLACK-EYED PEAS
8 CUPS WATER
2 BAY LEAVES
1 CUP LEMON JUICE
1 BUNCH PARSLEY, CHOPPED
3 TABLESPOONS SALT
1 TABLESPOON BLACK PEPPER
2 CUPS CANOLA OIL

1. In a saucepan, combine the black-eyed peas, water, and bay leaves. Bring to a boil, then reduce to a simmer. Cook until the beans are tender. Strain and cool.
2. Remove the bay leaves from the strained beans. In the bowl of a food processor, combine the cooked beans, lemon juice, parsley, salt, and pepper. Puree all ingredients together, slowly adding the oil until mixture reaches a smooth, silky consistency.

Veggie Burgers

1 ½ CUPS RED QUINOA, COOKED
4 CUPS RED KIDNEY BEANS, COOKED AND STRAINED
1 RED BELL PEPPER, CHOPPED
1 RED ONION, CHOPPED
2 PORTOBELLO MUSHROOMS, CHOPPED
4 CLOVES GARLIC
2 TABLESPOONS SALT
1 TABLESPOON BLACK PEPPER
1 TABLESPOON PAPRIKA
1 TEASPOON CRUSHED RED PEPPER
1 CUP PEPPER JACK CHEESE, SHREDDED
½ CUP FLOUR

1. Preheat the oven to 400°F.
2. In the bowl of a food processor, combine the quinoa and beans. Pulse together until a rough paste forms. Remove and set aside.
3. In the same bowl, chop the bell pepper, onion, mushrooms, garlic, and spices until a rough texture is reached. Add the cheese. Pulse until the mixture begins to thicken.
4. Add the quinoa-and-bean mixture to the vegetables. Pulse until a thick, tacky paste has formed. Transfer the mixture from the food processor to a separate bowl and fold in the flour.
5. Warm a nonstick griddle pan or a large, flat sauté pan on medium-high heat. Form the paste into burger-sized patties. Griddle each patty for 3 minutes on each side or until a crust is formed.
6. Transfer the patties to a parchment-lined sheet tray. Cook for 20 minutes. Remove from the oven.

Assembly

4 VEGGIE BURGERS
4 WHOLE WHEAT HAMBURGER BUNS, TOASTED
4 SLICES PEPPER JACK CHEESE
4 SLICES TOMATO
SEVERAL LEAVES OF ROMAINE LETTUCE
BLACK-EYED PEA HUMMUS

1. Place one hot burger on the bottom half of each bun. Place one slice of cheese on each burger. Top with tomato and lettuce.
2. Dress the top half of each bun with hummus. Place on the burger and serve.

TORTILLA SOUP

OIL, FOR FRYING
10 CORN TORTILLAS
¼ CUP CANOLA OIL
2 LARGE ONIONS, JULIENNED
1 TABLESPOON PLUS 3 TABLESPOONS SALT
1 TABLESPOON CUMIN
1 TABLESPOON PAPRIKA
1 TABLESPOON CHILI POWDER
2 TABLESPOONS BLACK PEPPER
1 BOTTLE (12 OUNCES) MEXICAN BEER
3 POUNDS ROMA TOMATOES, CHOPPED
3 ANCHO CHILES, STEMMED AND SEEDED
1 BUNCH CILANTRO, CHOPPED
2 QUARTS WATER
2 CUPS COOKED CHICKEN OR PORK, PULLED INTO STRIPS, FOR SERVING
QUESO FRESCO, FOR GARNISH

1. Deep-fry the corn tortillas until they're a deep, golden brown and very crisp. Set aside.
2. In a stock pot, heat the canola oil until it flows freely. Add the onions and 1 tablespoon salt. Sauté for 10 minutes, allowing the onions to char and deglazing occasionally with water to pull flavor from the bottom of the pot. When onions turn dark brown, add the 3 tablespoons salt and spices.
3. Deglaze one last time with the beer. Add the tomatoes, tortillas, ancho chiles, cilantro, and water. Bring to a boil, then let simmer 30 minutes.
4. Remove the pot from the heat. Using a blender, puree the ingredients to form a smooth, orange broth.
5. Place a small amount of chicken or pork in the bottom of each soup bowl. Ladle the hot soup over the meat. Garnish with queso fresco.

ALLEN JONAS'S MEXICAN CORN SOUP

2 TABLESPOONS BUTTER
2 SERRANO PEPPERS, SEEDED AND DICED
1 MEDIUM POBLANO CHILE, SEEDED AND DICED
1 CUP ONION, CHOPPED
¾ TEASPOON CUMIN
¾ TEASPOON OREGANO
1 14-OUNCE CAN WHOLE TOMATOES, CHOPPED
3 16-OUNCE CANS CREAMED CORN
1 ½ CUPS HALF-AND-HALF

1. Melt butter in soup pot.
2. Sauté peppers, chile, and onion for 10 minutes.
3. Add cumin, oregano, and tomatoes. Sauté 5 minutes.
4. Add corn and half-and-half. Cook over low heat until very warm, for approximately 20 minutes. Do not boil.

POTATO SALAD

4 LARGE RUSSET POTATOES, SKIN ON
1 EAR YELLOW CORN
1 YELLOW BELL PEPPER, DICED
2 STALKS CELERY, SLICED
2 TABLESPOONS PICKLED MUSTARD SEEDS (SEE RECIPE ON P. 214)
1 CUP MAYONNAISE
1 TABLESPOON PAPRIKA
1 TABLESPOON PLUS 1 TEASPOON SALT
1 TEASPOON BLACK PEPPER

1. Cut the potatoes into large chunks. Place in a stock pot, cover with cold water, and bring to a boil. Reduce to a simmer and cook until fork-tender. Strain and let cool.
2. On a grill or in a grill pan, char the corn until lightly blackened on all sides. Let cool, then cut the kernels from the cob.
3. Once the potatoes have cooled, thoroughly mix all ingredients together in a bowl. Let rest overnight to allow flavors to meld.
4. Allow salad to sit at room temperature 10 minutes prior to serving.

DINNER

It is no small order to serve a spectacular meal, night after night. For any culinary professional, let alone for a cooking enthusiast who doesn't view the task as a chore, having a nightly venue in which to display one's talent and creativity is a gift unlike any other. The opportunity to cook multicourse meals with relatively few restrictions is even better. Luckily for those willing and adept enough to cook during the hunting season, nights at Temple Ranch are just such occasions. Some guests have referred to their meals as "the best they have ever had."

In the earlier days of the ranch's history, meals weren't quite as structured or formal as they have become in the last few years. Cooks like Allen Jonas more or less stuck to a weekly menu of country favorites and stick-to-your-ribs fare, but he made enough of an impression on visitors that reminiscences of particular dishes can still be heard around the hot tub today. For this reason, Allen has generously contributed some of his enduring recipes to this book. Though things changed somewhat during my tenure, when I introduced dishes like coq au vin and paella, traditional meals such as meatloaf and fried chicken continued to be the most popular. As with other traditions on the ranch, old simply melded with the new.

What makes dinner at Temple Ranch so special holds true for the ranch itself. With each course, those cooking have the chance to create new memories that will eventually become old stories recounted for years to come. Like any day spent hunting or exploring the Rock House, dinner is not one stand-alone activity. Beginning with early evening hors d'oeuvres and ending with handcrafted desserts, dinner at Temple Ranch develops from course to course, telling its own story every night, just as the ranch has done for the last twenty years.

LOTTIE TEMPLE'S DUCK STEW

4 DUCKS
3 STALKS CELERY, CHOPPED
1 ONION, CHOPPED
2 TABLESPOONS PEQUÍN CHILE
¼ CUP SHERRY
4 BAY LEAVES
3 CUPS RICE
½ CUP BUTTER
1 TABLESPOON CAYENNE PEPPER
2 TABLESPOONS SALT
1 TABLESPOON BLACK PEPPER

1. In a large pot, combine the ducks, celery, onion, pequín chile, sherry, and bay leaves. Cover with water. Bring to a boil over high heat, then reduce to a simmer. Cook until ducks are tender, approximately 2 hours.
2. Remove ducks from broth and set aside to cool. Strain the broth and reserve.
3. When the ducks have cooled, remove all skin, fat, and bones. Pull the meat from the bones and shred. Set aside.
4. In a broad, shallow pot or rondo, combine the rice, butter, cayenne, salt, pepper, and 10 cups of the reserved broth. Bring to a boil, then reduce to a simmer over medium heat and cover. After 10 minutes, add the shredded duck. Let cook for 10 additional minutes. Serve hot.

MAY MAY DENMAN'S CHICKEN SPAGHETTI

Stock

4 QUARTS WATER
1 WHOLE CHICKEN, QUARTERED
3 STALKS CELERY, CHOPPED
3 CARROTS, CHOPPED
1 LEEK, WHITE PORTION ONLY, RINSED AND CHOPPED
1 BUNCH PARSLEY
2 BAY LEAVES
1 BUNCH SAGE
1 BUNCH THYME
1 BUNCH ROSEMARY
6 CLOVES GARLIC, WHOLE

1. Combine all ingredients in a large pot. Bring to a boil over high heat, then reduce to a simmer for 3 ½ hours.
2. Strain the broth into a container and reserve as stock. Set the chicken aside to cool, and discard the vegetables.
3. Once the chicken has cooled, remove the skin and bones. Reserve the meat.

Chicken Spaghetti

3 ½ QUARTS STOCK (APPROXIMATE)
1 28-OUNCE CAN WHOLE PEELED TOMATOES, WITH JUICE
1 POUND BUTTON MUSHROOMS, CHOPPED
1 ONION, CHOPPED
¼ CUP BUTTER
5 STALKS CELERY, CHOPPED
RESERVED CHICKEN MEAT
1 PACKAGE SPAGHETTI
2 TABLESPOONS SALT
1 TABLESPOON BLACK PEPPER
1 CUP GRATED CHEDDAR OR COLBY CHEESE, FOR SERVING

1. In a stock pot, combine the stock and tomatoes. Using your hands or a stick blender, chop the tomatoes until chunky. Bring to a simmer over medium heat.
2. In a sauté pan, sauté the mushrooms and onion in the butter until translucent. Add to the simmering broth with the celery, chicken, spaghetti, salt, and pepper.
3. Simmer over medium heat until the spaghetti has cooked and the broth has started to thicken.
4. Serve hot with grated cheese.

ALLEN JONAS'S PANKO-FRIED SHRIMP WITH TARTAR SAUCE

1 GALLON CANOLA OIL, FOR FRYING
4 CUPS FLOUR
2 TABLESPOONS PLUS 2 TABLESPOONS EMERIL'S ORIGINAL ESSENCE SEASONING
48 JUMBO SHRIMP, DEVEINED AND BUTTERFLIED
4 EGGS
½ CUP MILK
4 CUPS PANKO BREAD CRUMBS

1. Preheat oil to 325°F for frying.
2. Combine the flour and 2 tablespoons Emeril's seasoning. Dredge the shrimp in the mixture until thoroughly coated. Shake off excess.
3. In a bowl, mix together the eggs and the milk to make a wash. Dip the dredged shrimp in the wash. Shake off excess.
4. In a separate bowl, combine the panko and remaining 2 tablespoons Emeril's seasoning. Dredge shrimp until fully coated. Shake off excess.
5. Fry shrimp until golden. Serve hot with Allen Jonas's Tartar Sauce (see recipe on p. 216).

ALLEN JONAS'S CARNE GUISADA

4 CUPS FLOUR
1 TABLESPOON SALT
2 TABLESPOONS BLACK PEPPER
6 POUNDS TENDERIZED ROUND STEAK, TRIMMED OF ALL FAT AND CUT INTO LARGE PIECES
LARD OR OIL, FOR FRYING
10 TO 14 OUNCES WATER
6 TABLESPOONS FIESTA BRAND CARNE GUISADA SEASONING
4 HEAPING TABLESPOONS CORNSTARCH
RICE

1. Combine the flour, salt, and pepper.
2. Dredge meat in the mixture until thoroughly coated. Shake off excess.
3. Warm lard or oil over medium-high heat in a large skillet, and fry meat in batches until evenly brown. Remove to drain on paper towels. Discard grease.
4. Add water to skillet and scrape loose the drippings. (Be careful to remove any burned pieces.)
5. Cut meat into bite-size pieces and place in large (10- or 12-quart) pot.
6. Pour water from skillet into the pot, enough to cover meat about 2 inches.
7. Add 2 tablespoons carne guisada seasoning and cook until tender (approximately 1 hour), stirring occasionally.
8. In a separate bowl, add water to cornstarch. Pour into pot with remaining carne guisada seasoning. Cook just until incorporated. Add more water if needed to achieve desired consistency.
9. Serve over rice.

CHICKEN-FRIED VENISON

1 VENISON BACKSTRAP, BRINED (SEE BRINE RECIPE ON P. 213)
2 CUPS FLOUR
1 TABLESPOON SALT
1 TABLESPOON BLACK PEPPER
1 TABLESPOON CUMIN
2 TEASPOONS CHILI POWDER
2 TEASPOONS PAPRIKA
4 EGGS
2 CUPS WHOLE MILK
1 QUART CANOLA OIL, FOR FRYING

1. In a container with a lid, combine the backstrap with brine. Brine for 2 days.
2. Remove the venison from the brine and pat dry with paper towels. Cut into 1-inch-thick slices. Use a meat mallet to pound the slices thin, to roughly twice their original size. Set aside.
3. In a large bowl, combine the flour, salt, pepper, cumin, chili powder, and paprika. Mix well.
4. In a separate bowl, beat together the eggs and milk.
5. Dip each piece of flattened venison into the egg mixture with one hand. Once the venison is covered in egg mixture, dredge it in the seasoned flour, using the other hand to cover it completely. Shake off excess flour.
6. In a large sauté pan, heat 2 cups of the oil to 350°F. Immerse the breaded pieces of venison in the hot oil. Cook until golden brown.
7. Remove cooked venison and set on a wire rack. Serve hot.

GRILLED VENISON

1 VENISON BACKSTRAP, BRINED (SEE BRINE RECIPE ON P. 213)

Grilling
1 TABLESPOON SALT
1 TABLESPOON BLACK PEPPER
¼ CUP CANOLA OIL

1. In a container with a lid, combine the backstrap with brine. Brine for 2 days.
2. Heat the grill to 400°F. Remove the venison from the brine and pat dry. Season with salt and pepper. Drizzle with the canola oil to prevent sticking on the grill.
3. Place the venison on the grill and cook to medium rare, approximately 15 minutes (time will vary depending on both the grill and the size of the backstrap).
4. Remove and let rest 10 minutes. Serve warm.

ALLEN JONAS'S DRUNK-AND-DIRTY BEEF TENDERLOIN WITH CREAMY HORSERADISH SAUCE

Marinade

1 CUP SOY SAUCE
½ CUP BOURBON
¼ CUP WORCESTERSHIRE SAUCE
2 TABLESPOONS DARK BROWN SUGAR
½ TEASPOON POWDERED GINGER
4 CLOVES GARLIC, MINCED

Beef Tenderloin

2 POUNDS BEEF TENDERLOIN
2 TABLESPOONS COARSE-GROUND BLACK PEPPER
1 TEASPOON WHITE PEPPER
¼ CUP OIL, PREFERABLY CANOLA OR CORN

1. Combine the marinade ingredients. Place the whole tenderloin in a shallow dish and pour the mixture over the meat. Marinate the tenderloin for 4 to 8 hours in the refrigerator, turning occasionally.
2. Take the meat from the refrigerator. Marinate 1 hour at room temperature. Keep the temperature steady at approximately 200°F. Meanwhile, start a fire in the pit.
3. Remove the tenderloin from the marinade. Cover it thoroughly with first the black pepper, then the white pepper. Over high heat in a skillet (on the stove or on a hot outdoor grill), sear the meat several seconds on every side.
4. Split the marinade into two equal portions, and set one half aside. In a saucepan over high heat, bring the other half of the marinade to a boil, then add the oil. Use the mixture as a mop sauce, applying it to the meat every 15 to 20 minutes during the smoking process.

5. Place the meat in the pit and cook it at 180°F to 220°F, until the internal temperature of the meat reaches 140°F, approximately 1 ½ to 2 hours. (Use an instant-read meat thermometer to check for doneness. Be careful not to overcook; tenderloin is always best rare to medium-rare.)
6. Remove the tenderloin from the pit and let it sit 15 minutes before slicing. In the meantime, put the unused portion of marinade in a small, heavy saucepan, bring it to a boil, and reduce to a simmer. Cook for 5 to 10 minutes, until the marinade is reduced by one-quarter.
7. Slice the tenderloin and serve it with the sauce (on the side) and with Creamy Horseradish Sauce (recipe follows).

Creamy Horseradish Sauce

1 8-OUNCE PACKAGE CREAM CHEESE
½ CUP PREPARED HORSERADISH
¼ CUP MAYONNAISE
¼ CUP STONEGROUND DIJON MUSTARD

1. Combine all ingredients in a mixing bowl. Use an electric mixer on high speed to blend for 1 to 2 minutes or until sauce is smooth and creamy.
2. Keep covered and chilled until ready to use.

CARNIVORE SPECIAL

Imagine fifteen men left to their own devices on a hunting weekend, and the Carnivore Special becomes a very real meal option. Less a recipe and more a celebration of grilling, manhood, and the spoils of a weekend in the country, this simple meal has been a staple of the stag hunts at Temple Ranch for the last twenty years. There are very few steps involved, so it's a cinch to cook and clean up. Its assembly is simple: Meat. Grill. Serve.

A SAMPLING OF YOUR FAVORITE MEATS, SUCH AS PORK RIBS, PORK CHOPS, SIRLOIN STEAKS, SAUSAGES, AND CHICKEN
SALT
SPICES (CAYENNE PEPPER, CHILI POWDER, PAPRIKA, ETC.)
POTATOES AND/OR OTHER VEGETABLES

1. Build a fire in the grill using hardwood such as mesquite (the Texas favorite), oak, or hickory.
2. Season, marinade, or otherwise treat meat as desired. Then place meat—along with potatoes and other vegetables—on the hot grill and cook to desired doneness. (If cooking ribs, season generously with salt and spices, then cook for 3 to 4 hours on the cool part of the grill.)
3. Serve hot.

BEEF TENDERLOIN WITH GRILLED ASPARAGUS AND BACON-GORGONZOLA SAUCE

Beef and Asparagus

6 6-OUNCE BEEF TENDERLOIN FILETS
2 TABLESPOONS PLUS 2 TEASPOONS SALT
2 TEASPOONS PLUS 1 TEASPOON BLACK PEPPER
½ CUP PLUS ¼ CUP CANOLA OIL
2 BUNCHES GREEN ASPARAGUS

1. Heat a grill to 400°F. Season the filets generously with 2 tablespoons salt and 2 teaspoons pepper, then lightly coat in ½ cup canola oil.
2. Coat the asparagus with ¼ cup canola oil, 2 teaspoons salt, and 1 teaspoon pepper. Set aside.
3. Grill the tenderloins to the desired temperature (approximately 5 minutes on each side for medium-rare). Remove from the grill and set aside.
4. Add the asparagus to the hot grill and cook 2 minutes. Flip and cook 2 more minutes, until lightly charred.
5. Serve hot with Bacon-Gorgonzola Sauce (recipe follows).

Bacon-Gorgonzola Sauce

5 STRIPS APPLEWOOD-SMOKED BACON, THICK CUT
1 CLOVE GARLIC, MINCED
2 CUPS HEAVY CREAM
1 ½ CUPS GORGONZOLA, CRUMBLED

1. Cut the strips of bacon into small chunks, approximately ¼ inch wide.
2. In a nonstick pan, cook the bacon over high heat until dark brown and crisp. Pour off the rendered fat. Add the garlic and cook 1 minute.
3. Pour in the cream and allow to come just to a boil. Reduce heat to medium and add the Gorgonzola. Cook over medium heat until a thick, gravy-like texture has been reached.
4. Serve hot over the beef and asparagus.

FRIED FISH AND DIRTY RICE

Fried Fish

OIL, FOR FRYING
3 POUNDS RED DRUM (OR SIMILAR FLAKY WHITE FISH), SKINNED AND DEBONED
1 CUP RICE FLOUR
1 CUP WONDRA FLOUR
1 CUP ALL-PURPOSE FLOUR
1 BOTTLE (12 OUNCES) HEINEKEN, OR SIMILAR LIGHT BEER
1 12-OUNCE BOTTLE SPARKLING WATER
2 TABLESPOONS SALT
2 TEASPOONS BLACK PEPPER
1 TEASPOON GROUND GINGER
1 TEASPOON PAPRIKA

1. Pour the oil into a pot, ensuring at least a 2-inch gap between the top of the oil and the rim of the pot. Using a candy or fryer thermometer, heat oil to 375°F.
2. Portion the fish into 4-ounce filets.
3. Combine all other ingredients in a bowl. Whisk together until no lumps remain in the batter.
4. Immerse each filet in the batter until it is covered. Slowly place each battered filet in the hot oil. Fry for 6 minutes, or until the crust is a rich, golden brown. Serve hot with Scratch Tartar Sauce (see recipe on p. 216).

Dirty Rice

2 LINKS SPANISH-STYLE CHORIZO
2 TABLESPOONS CANOLA OIL
1 RED ONION, DICED
2 CLOVES GARLIC, MINCED
4 TEASPOONS SALT
1 TEASPOON BLACK PEPPER
2 TEASPOONS GROUND TURMERIC
½ TEASPOON CAYENNE PEPPER
1 TEASPOON PAPRIKA
2 CUPS LONG-GRAIN WHITE RICE
4 ½ CUPS WATER

1. Cut the chorizo into ¼-inch-thick rounds. Set aside.
2. In a 6-quart saucepan, heat the canola oil until it flows freely. Add the onion, garlic, and chorizo. Sauté 3 minutes.
3. Add the spices and rice. Sauté until the spices have been evenly incorporated and the rice has been lightly glazed with oil.
4. Add the water. Bring to a boil, and cook on high heat until a thin layer of liquid remains on top of the rice.
5. Reduce to low and cover. Cook for 8 minutes, then immediately remove from heat. Serve hot.

JOHN HANNAH'S NEW YEAR'S MEMORIAL LAMB AND NEW POTATOES

Lamb

1 BUNCH PARSLEY
2 TABLESPOONS ROSEMARY LEAVES
½ RED ONION, JULIENNED
1 TABLESPOON MUSTARD
3 CLOVES GARLIC
¼ CUP LEMON JUICE
1 TABLESPOON SALT
1 TABLESPOON BLACK PEPPER
12 LAMB RIB CHOPS

1. In the bowl of a food processor, combine the parsley, rosemary, onion, mustard, garlic, lemon juice, salt, and pepper. Puree until smooth.
2. Remove the marinade from the food processor and liberally cover the lamb chops. Let marinate between 2 and 24 hours (the longer the marinade, the deeper the flavor).
3. Grill the marinated chops over a hot grill for approximately 3 minutes on each side, or until the marinade has charred. Serve hot with New Potatoes (recipe follows).

New Potatoes

2 POUNDS NEW POTATOES
¼ CUP OLIVE OIL
1 TABLESPOON SALT
1 TEASPOON BLACK PEPPER

1. Preheat the oven to 400°F. Season the potatoes with the oil, salt, and pepper. Roast until tender, approximately 25 minutes.
2. Remove from the oven and serve hot.

GRILLED QUAIL WITH WHITE BEANS, MUSHROOMS, AND ARUGULA

Quail

1 BUNCH PARSLEY
2 CLOVES GARLIC
½ RED ONION, JULIENNED
⅓ CUP WHITE BALSAMIC VINEGAR
2 TABLESPOONS HONEY
1 TABLESPOON MUSTARD
1 TABLESPOON SALT
2 TEASPOONS BLACK PEPPER
1 CUP CANOLA OIL
8 SEMI-BONELESS QUAIL

1. Warm the grill to 400°F.
2. In the bowl of a food processor, combine the parsley, garlic, onion, vinegar, honey, mustard, and spices. Process until smooth. Then slowly drizzle the canola oil into the mixture so a smooth, glossy marinade is formed.
3. Marinate the quail for 2 hours.
4. Grill the quail approximately 4 minutes per side. Serve hot atop White Beans, Mushrooms, and Arugula (recipe follows).

White Beans, Mushrooms, and Arugula

2 CUPS CANNELLINI BEANS
10 CUPS WATER
1 TABLESPOON PLUS 1 TEASPOON SALT
1 BAY LEAF
½ CUP PLUS 2 TABLESPOONS BUTTER
2 TABLESPOONS CANOLA OIL
1 POUND OYSTER MUSHROOMS, CLEANED
1 TABLESPOON BLACK PEPPER
2 CUPS ARUGULA

1. Place the beans, water, 1 tablespoon salt, and bay leaf in a saucepan. Bring to a boil, then lower to a simmer. Cook until the beans are tender, approximately 1 ½ hours.
2. Strain off excess liquid so the beans are just covered. Keep warm.
3. In a pan over high heat, melt the ½ cup butter and the canola oil. Add the mushrooms. Sauté 5 minutes.
4. Add the contents of the mushroom pan to the beans along with the remaining 2 tablespoons butter, 1 teaspoon salt, and pepper. Cook over low heat until the butter has melted.
5. Fold the arugula into the hot beans until it wilts. Serve immediately.

MEATLOAF WITH MASHED POTATOES AND CREAM GRAVY

Meatloaf

1 28-OUNCE CAN WHOLE, PEELED TOMATOES, INCLUDING LIQUID
2 TABLESPOONS PLUS 3 TABLESPOONS WORCESTERSHIRE SAUCE
2 TEASPOONS PLUS 3 TABLESPOONS SALT
2 TABLESPOONS CANOLA OIL
1 ONION, DICED
2 POUNDS GRASS-FED GROUND BEEF
2 POUNDS GROUND PORK
2 EGGS
1 12-OUNCE BOTTLE SPARKLING WATER
1 CUP BREAD CRUMBS
1 TABLESPOON BLACK PEPPER
⅓ CUP WATER

1. Preheat the oven to 350°F.
2. In the bowl of a food processor, puree the peeled tomatoes, 2 tablespoons Worcestershire sauce, and 2 teaspoons salt until smooth. Set aside.
3. In a sauté pan, warm the canola oil over high heat until it flows freely. Add the onion and sauté for 8 minutes. Deglaze once with water and cook until lightly browned. Remove from heat and set aside to cool.
4. In a large mixing bowl, mix together the beef, pork, eggs, water, bread crumbs, 3 tablespoons Worcestershire sauce, 3 tablespoons salt, pepper, and the sautéed onions. Mix thoroughly so all the ingredients are evenly incorporated.
5. In a large (approximately 10 × 15-inch) baking dish, form the meat mixture into a loaf shape, making sure to leave space between the loaf and dish walls to allow for sauce to cover. Pour the pureed tomato sauce over the top. Cover in foil.
6. Roast at 350°F for 45 minutes. Remove the foil and turn the oven to 400°F. Roast for an additional 15 minutes, until the tomatoes have begun to form a crust.
7. Remove the meatloaf from the oven and let rest 15 minutes. Slice into 1-½-inch-thick slices. Serve warm with Mashed Potatoes and Cream Gravy (recipes follow).

Mashed Potatoes

4 POUNDS CREAMER OR YUKON GOLD POTATOES, SKIN ON
3 CLOVES GARLIC
2 CUPS HEAVY CREAM
1 CUP BUTTER, SOFTENED
¼ CUP OLIVE OIL
2 TABLESPOONS SALT
2 TEASPOONS BLACK PEPPER

1. Cut each potato into large chunks and place in a stock pot. Add the garlic. Fill the pot with cold water to just cover the potatoes. Bring the water to a boil, then reduce to a simmer until the potatoes are fork-tender, approximately 25 minutes.
2. In a small pot, cook the heavy cream over low heat until warm.
3. Remove the cooked potatoes from heat and strain. Place the warm potatoes in a large mixing bowl. Add the butter, olive oil, salt, and pepper. Using a hand mixer (not turned on), mash the potato mixture.
4. Add ½ cup of the heavy cream and begin to blend with the mixer. Continue adding cream slowly until the potatoes have been whipped to a thick, silky texture with a few lumps remaining. Serve hot.

Cream Gravy

½ CUP BUTTER
½ CUP FLOUR
1 QUART HEAVY CREAM
1 TABLESPOON SALT
2 TEASPOONS BLACK PEPPER

1. In a saucepan, melt the butter over high heat. Add the flour and whisk constantly until mixture forms a gritty paste with a nutty aroma, approximately 4 minutes.
2. Pour in the cream, salt, and pepper. Stir constantly until the cream has thickened to a gravy, approximately 5 minutes.
3. Serve hot over Mashed Potatoes.

CHILES RELLENOS WITH REFRIED BEANS AND MOLE

Prepare chiles and filling at least two hours in advance of assembly.

Chiles Rellenos

8 POBLANO CHILES
¼ CUP PLUS ¼ CUP PLUS ¼ CUP CANOLA OIL
1 TABLESPOON PLUS 1 TABLESPOON PLUS 2 TABLESPOONS SALT
1 TABLESPOON PLUS 1 TEASPOON PLUS 2 TEASPOONS BLACK PEPPER
1 ½ POUNDS CHICKEN THIGHS, BONELESS AND SKINLESS
1 TEASPOON CUMIN
1 TEASPOON PAPRIKA
2 TEASPOONS TAJÍN (MEXICAN LIME SALT)
½ ONION, DICED
2 CUPS LONG-GRAIN WHITE RICE
4 ½ CUPS WATER
2 CUPS MILD, CREAMY CHEESE LIKE COLBY JACK, SHREDDED
1 BUNCH CILANTRO, CHOPPED
1 CUP QUESO FRESCO, FOR GARNISH

Chiles

1. Heat grill or griddle to 400°F. In a bowl, toss the poblano peppers with ¼ cup canola oil, 1 tablespoon salt, and 1 tablespoon pepper. Place the chiles on the hot grill. Turn frequently until charred evenly (but not to ash).
2. Remove chiles from the grill and place in a sealed plastic container or a bowl covered in plastic. Allow to cool completely while covered.
3. Peel the skin from each chile. Using the tip of a knife, gently slice each chile open on one side only. Remove the seeds without tearing other sides of the chile. Set aside.

Chicken

1. Preheat the oven to 400°F. In a bowl, season the chicken with ¼ cup canola oil, 1 tablespoon salt, and 1 teaspoon pepper; add cumin, paprika, and Tajín. Roast for 20 minutes, until cooked through. Remove and let cool.
2. Once cool, cut the chicken into thin strips. Set aside.

Rice

1. In a 6-quart saucepan, warm ¼ cup canola oil over high heat until it flows freely. Add the onion and 2 tablespoons salt. Sauté 2 minutes until translucent.
2. Add the rice and 2 teaspoons pepper. Sauté until the rice is evenly coated with oil.
3. Add the water and boil the rice until a thin layer of liquid remains on top. Reduce heat to low and cover. Cook for 8 minutes, then immediately remove from heat.
4. Pour into a pan and cool. Set aside.

Assembly

1. Preheat the oven to 350°F.
2. In a bowl, combine the cooked rice, chopped chicken, shredded cheese, and cilantro. Then begin squeezing the mixture by hand until clumps start to form. As the warmth of your hands melts the cheese, the mixture will form clumps that don't fall apart. Shape the rice mixture into balls, each roughly the size of a tennis ball.
3. Place each ball into a peeled and seeded chile. Slowly press the rice mixture into the skin of the chile, using the chile's shape to determine the amount of filling. Stuff each chile until the skin can wrap around the rice and the two sides meet, but do not push hard enough to rip the chile.
4. Place the chiles next to one another in a baking dish, seam down and tightly packed. Cover the dish in foil and roast for 45 minutes. Remove the foil. Let cook for an additional 15 minutes.
5. Remove the dish from the oven and uncover. Let cool for 15 minutes, then serve each chile on top of the Refried Beans, covered in Mole (recipes follow). Garnish with queso fresco.

Refried Beans

¼ CUP PLUS 1 CUP CANOLA OIL
1 ONION, DICED
1 TABLESPOON CHILI POWDER
1 TABLESPOON PAPRIKA
2 TABLESPOONS SALT
2 TEASPOONS BLACK PEPPER
2 CUPS PINTO BEANS
9 CUPS WATER

1. In a large pot, heat ¼ cup canola oil until it flows freely. Sauté the onion and spices for 2 minutes or until translucent.
2. Add the beans and water. Bring to a boil, then reduce to a simmer. Cook until beans are tender, approximately 1 ½ hours. Remove from heat and let cool, then strain.
3. Place the strained beans in the bowl of a food processor. Blend with 1 cup canola oil.
4. Return the pureed beans to a pot. Cook over low heat until warm. Serve with Chiles Rellenos.

Mole

Mole is one of those sauces that should never be made in small batches. Its soul rests in long cooking and lots of flavors that come together to form a sauce unlike any other. This batch will yield quite a bit, and if you're a fan of Mexican food, it can be used in many different applications. Any leftovers can be frozen in individual batches and thawed again for single uses.

OIL, FOR FRYING
5 CORN TORTILLAS
6 BANANAS
1 CUP CANOLA OIL
5 YELLOW ONIONS, JULIENNED
¼ CUP SALT
4 CUPS DRIED GUAJILLO CHILES, STEMMED AND SEEDED
4 CUPS DRIED ANCHO CHILES, STEMMED AND SEEDED
12 OUNCES RAW PUMPKIN SEEDS
1 7-OUNCE PACK GRAHAM CRACKERS
1 DISC ABUELITA CHOCOLATE
1 QUART PLUS 8 QUARTS WATER
SALT AND BLACK PEPPER TO TASTE

1. Using a deep fryer, fry the tortillas until dark brown and crispy. Fry the bananas until golden brown. Set aside.
2. In a large stock pot, heat the canola oil until it flows freely. Add the onions and salt. Sauté until onions are deep brown, approximately 15 minutes, deglazing frequently with up to 1 quart water when they begin to char.
3. Add the chiles. Sauté until aroma is released, approximately 10 minutes. Add the pumpkin seeds and sauté for 2 more minutes.
4. Add the fried tortillas, fried bananas, graham crackers, chocolate, and remaining 8 quarts water. Bring to a boil, then reduce to a simmer and cook 1 hour.
5. Remove from heat. Using a blender, puree all the ingredients on high speed until very smooth.
6. Return pureed sauce to the pot. Cook over medium heat until reduced by one-quarter. Season to taste. Serve hot with Chiles Rellenos and other recipes.

PAPPARDELLE ALFREDO WITH CHICKEN

16 OUNCES DRIED ARTISAN PAPPARDELLE
6 CHICKEN BREASTS, BONELESS AND SKINLESS
2 TABLESPOONS PLUS 3 TABLESPOONS OLIVE OIL
1 TABLESPOON PLUS 1 TABLESPOON SALT
½ TEASPOON PLUS 1 TEASPOON BLACK PEPPER
½ ONION, DICED
4 CLOVES GARLIC, MINCED
1 QUART HEAVY CREAM
1 ½ CUPS PARMESAN, SHREDDED
½ CUP PARSLEY, CHOPPED

1. Preheat the oven to 400°F. Season the chicken breasts with 2 tablespoons olive oil, 1 tablespoon salt, and ½ teaspoon pepper. Roast for 20 minutes, until cooked through. Remove from oven and set aside.
2. Cook the pappardelle per the manufacturer's instructions. Lightly oil to prevent sticking and set aside.
3. Meanwhile, in a 6-quart saucepan, warm 3 tablespoons olive oil over high heat until it flows freely. Sauté the onion and 1 tablespoon salt for 3 minutes, until translucent. Add the garlic and cook for 1 minute.
4. Pour in the heavy cream. Cook until it just begins to bubble rapidly, then reduce to medium heat. Whisk in the Parmesan and 1 teaspoon pepper. Cook over medium heat until the sauce thickens to a gravy-like consistency. Add the cooked pasta to the sauce, ensuring that all the noodles are generously coated.
5. Serve the pasta hot on a plate, topped with the roasted chicken. Garnish with the chopped parsley.

FRIED CHICKEN WITH MASHED POTATOES AND CHARRED AGAVE-BUTTERED CORN

Fried Chicken

1 POUND CHICKEN LEGS, SKIN ON
1 POUND CHICKEN BREASTS, BONELESS AND SKINLESS
1 POUND CHICKEN THIGHS, BONE IN AND SKIN ON
1 QUART BUTTERMILK
2 TABLESPOONS BLACK PEPPERCORNS
1 TABLESPOON PLUS 3 TABLESPOONS SALT
1 TABLESPOON PLUS 1 TABLESPOON CUMIN
1 CUP RICE FLOUR
1 CUP WONDRA FLOUR
1 CUP ALL-PURPOSE FLOUR
2 TABLESPOONS BLACK PEPPER
OIL, FOR FRYING

1. Place the chicken pieces in a container with a lid. Pour the buttermilk over the chicken. Add the peppercorns, 1 tablespoon salt, and 1 tablespoon cumin. Mix until the chicken pieces are covered entirely. Let marinate overnight.
2. Heat the frying oil to 375°F (measure with a candy or frying thermometer).
3. In a large mixing bowl, mix together the rice flour, Wondra flour, and all-purpose flour with the pepper, the remaining 3 tablespoons salt, and 1 tablespoon cumin.
4. Remove the chicken one piece at a time from the marinade. Dredge generously in the flour until thoroughly covered, then shake off excess. Slowly immerse each piece in the hot oil. Cook the breasts and thighs for 15 minutes, the legs for 12 minutes.
5. Remove the chicken from the hot oil and let drain over a wire rack. Serve hot with Mashed Potatoes (see recipe on p. 140) and Charred Agave-Buttered Corn.

Charred Agave-Buttered Corn

1 CUP BUTTER, SOFTENED
¼ CUP AGAVE NECTAR
1 TEASPOON SALT
4 EARS YELLOW CORN

1. In the bowl of a stand mixer, combine the butter, agave nectar, and salt. Using the paddle attachment, beat together until the agave has been fully incorporated.
2. Place the whipped butter mixture in a dish and refrigerate 2 hours.
3. Heat a grill to 400°F. Cut each ear of corn in half, then place directly on the grill. Cook until the corn has been lightly charred on all sides.
4. Serve warm with the chilled agave butter.

CREAMED CORN

3 TABLESPOONS CANOLA OIL
1 ONION, DICED
1 RED BELL PEPPER
1 TABLESPOON SALT
6 EARS YELLOW CORN, KERNELS CUT FROM THE COB
1 TEASPOON BLACK PEPPER
2 TEASPOONS PAPRIKA
2 CUPS HEAVY CREAM
½ CUP BUTTER

1. In a sauté pan, heat the canola oil until it flows freely. Sauté the onion, bell pepper, and salt for 3 minutes, or until translucent.
2. Add the corn, black pepper, and paprika. Sauté for 5 minutes, until the corn begins to pop and is glazed with the oil.
3. Add the cream and cook on high heat until it barely bubbles (be careful not to break the cream). Reduce heat to medium-low and simmer until the cream reduces by half.
4. Add the butter. Once the butter has melted, serve hot.

BEEF LASAGNA

1 BOX (12 TO 15) ARTISANAL LASAGNA NOODLES
¼ CUP CANOLA OIL
2 CARROTS, DICED
1 ONION, DICED
2 TABLESPOONS SALT
1 TABLESPOON BLACK PEPPER
2 TABLESPOONS ROSEMARY LEAVES, MINCED
1 TABLESPOON THYME LEAVES, MINCED
2 POUNDS 85% LEAN GRASS-FED GROUND BEEF
2 16-OUNCE BALLS FRESH MOZZARELLA
6 CUPS TOMATO SAUCE (SEE RECIPE ON P. 80)
1 22-OUNCE CONTAINER WHOLE MILK RICOTTA
1 CUP PARMESAN, FRESHLY GRATED

1. Cook the lasagna per the manufacturer's instructions, until al dente. Strain and separate individually. Lightly oil to prevent sticking and set aside.
2. In a sauté pan, warm canola oil over high heat until it flows freely. Add the carrots, onion, salt, and pepper. Sauté for 3 minutes, until the onions are translucent. Add the herbs. Cook for 1 minute.
3. Add the ground beef and reduce the heat to medium. Cook the beef completely through, stirring frequently. Remove pan from heat.
4. Cut each ball of mozzarella in half and then into ¼-inch-thick slices. Set each sliced ball aside separately.

Assembly

1. Preheat the oven to 350°F. Ladle a small amount of tomato sauce into the bottom of a 9 × 13-inch baking dish to form a light layer.
2. Cover the sauce with 3 or 4 noodles, laid side by side, just overlapping. Using a slotted spoon, cover the noodles with half of the cooked ground beef mixture.
3. Layer one ball of the mozzarella slices over the ground beef. Drop ricotta into the spaces between mozzarella slices, and spread with a spatula to form an even layer. Cover the cheese layer with 2 cups of sauce.
4. Repeat steps 2 and 3.
5. Top the sauce with the remaining noodles. Cover those noodles with the remaining sauce. Sprinkle the Parmesan over the sauce.
6. Bake for 30 minutes. Rotate the dish and raise the heat to 400°F. Bake for 15 more minutes, until the Parmesan has begun to melt into the sauce on top.
7. Remove the lasagna from the oven. Let cool for 15 minutes before serving.

POLENTA

This is best cooked in a thick-bottomed saucepan to prevent charring. To reheat left-over polenta, cover the bottom of a pot with whole milk and place polenta in the pot. Cook over low heat until the polenta has loosened up and is warm.

¼ CUP CANOLA OIL
½ ONION, DICED
½ CUP BUTTER
2 CUPS COARSE CORNMEAL
7 CUPS BOILING WATER
1 CUP HEAVY CREAM
8 OUNCES CHÈVRE (GOAT CHEESE)
¼ CUP LEMON JUICE
3 TABLESPOONS SALT

1. In a saucepan, warm the canola oil over high heat until it flows freely. Add the onion and sauté for 3 minutes, until translucent. Add the butter and cook until it melts completely.
2. Add the cornmeal, toasting until it is completely saturated, approximately 2 minutes.
3. Ladle the boiling water into the pan until the cornmeal is covered by double the amount of water. Whisk briskly until the cornmeal begins to thicken. Once the cornmeal has absorbed the water and begins to bubble, reduce heat to medium-low. (Be careful! The boiling cornmeal will result in painful burns if it touches your skin.)
4. Cook the polenta over medium-low heat until the coarse texture of the cornmeal has softened, approximately 1 hour, stirring frequently. If the polenta becomes too thick, add hot water little by little to thin it out.
5. Stir the heavy cream, goat cheese, lemon juice, and salt into the polenta. Once the cheese has melted, serve hot.

GREEN BEAN CASSEROLE

3 TABLESPOONS CANOLA OIL
1 ONION, JULIENNED
1 TABLESPOON SALT
2 CUPS MUSHROOMS, SLICED
1 POUND FRESH GREEN BEANS, STEMMED
2 TEASPOONS BLACK PEPPER
2 CUPS HEAVY CREAM
1 16-OUNCE CAN FRIED ONIONS

1. Preheat the oven to 375°F.
2. In a large sauté pan, warm the canola oil over high heat until it flows freely. Sauté the onion and salt for 3 minutes, until translucent.
3. Add the mushrooms, green beans, and black pepper. Sauté for 3 minutes.
4. Pour the cream into the pan and allow to barely boil. Reduce heat to medium and cook until the cream has thickened to a gravy-like consistency.
5. Pour the green bean mixture into a serving dish and garnish with the fried onions. Bake for 15 minutes. Remove and serve hot.

ROASTED VEGETABLES

Serve these alongside any dish, or simply dress a plate with 1 tablespoon Fresh Aioli (see recipe on p. 215) and top with the roasted vegetables. Or, for a delicious salad, dress fresh arugula with 2 tablespoons Cider-Vanilla Vinaigrette (see recipe on p. 215) and top with roasted vegetables.

1 HEAD BROCCOLI, CUT INTO LARGE FLORETS
1 HEAD CAULIFLOWER, CUT INTO LARGE FLORETS
1 POUND BRUSSELS SPROUTS, CUT LENGTHWISE INTO HALVES
½ CUP OLIVE OIL
1 TABLESPOON SALT
1 TEASPOON BLACK PEPPER

1. Preheat the oven to 400°F.
2. Mix all ingredients together in a bowl, then spread evenly on a sheet pan. Roast for 20 minutes, until the cauliflower and broccoli begin to char. Serve warm.

DESSERT

It goes without saying that much more happens behind the scenes at a restaurant or resort than guests will ever know. Quick hands can often cover up mistakes that would have otherwise ruined an entire occasion. Mistakes, too, can often become happy accidents that guests remember for years to come. For chefs, though, one of the perpetual behind-the-scenes battles is dessert, the course that some people anticipate more than any other.

It is not that savory chefs are incapable of assembling delicious combinations of sugar, cream, butter, and flour to make a respectable dessert; it is more often the case that they just dread the task. For private chefs, it is understood that dessert must become part of their repertoire if they are to succeed at an assignment. Some despise the necessity of making dessert so much that they will buy something premade just to avoid the hassle. Others accept the challenge and amaze their guests from the first to the last bite.

As with the recipes throughout this book, the following dessert recipes have stood the test of time. For the Temples, some are new classics that have become part of their culinary memories in the last couple of years. Whether a new favorite or a tried-and-true classic, the desserts here represent how the food served at Temple Ranch has so thoroughly evolved in the last twenty years, from something rustic and simple to something that, occasionally, looks almost too good to eat.

CHOCOLATE-ORANGE MOUSSE WITH CINNAMON SHORTBREAD COOKIES

2 CUPS HEAVY CREAM
10 OUNCES DARK CHOCOLATE CHIPS
1 TABLESPOON CINNAMON
¼ CUP ORANGE JUICE
4 EGGS
2 TABLESPOONS SUGAR
ZEST OF 1 ORANGE

1. In a bowl, using a hand mixer or a stand mixer, whip the cream until it forms light peaks. Reserve cold in the refrigerator.
2. Using a double boiler (a metal bowl placed over a simmering pot of water), melt the chocolate with the cinnamon.
3. While the chocolate is melting, warm the orange juice in a small saucepan over medium heat until just warm. In a separate bowl, beat together the eggs and sugar until light and fluffy.
4. Stir the warm orange juice quickly into the melted chocolate (still over the double boiler), making sure to stir constantly because the chocolate will want to harden. Remove the metal bowl from the boiler and stir in the whipped eggs and orange zest until fully incorporated.
5. Using a large spatula, gently fold the whipped cream into the chocolate mixture until fully incorporated. Refrigerate the mousse in a large dish until firm (up to 6 hours), or portion into smaller dishes and refrigerate individually.
6. Serve with Cinnamon Shortbread Cookies (recipe follows).

Cinnamon Shortbread Cookies

This cookie dough is super-firm and requires use of a stand mixer.

1 CUP BUTTER, SOFTENED
½ CUP SUGAR
1 EGG
½ TABLESPOON VANILLA EXTRACT
2 CUPS FLOUR
2 TEASPOONS CINNAMON
1 TEASPOON SALT

1. In the bowl of a stand mixer, cream together the butter and sugar. Slowly beat in the egg.
2. Add the vanilla, flour, cinnamon, and salt. Beat until fully incorporated.
3. Remove the dough from the bowl and spread in a horizontal line on a sheet of parchment or wax paper. Fold the bottom and top of the paper over the dough until both sides of the paper are touching. Press the paper against the dough and gently squeeze the dough out toward the edges of the paper until a semi-round log has formed. Reposition the log at one end of the paper, and roll the log into the paper. Twist the ends shut. Freeze until firm, approximately 1 hour.
4. Preheat the oven to 350°F.
5. Remove the dough from the freezer and cut into ¼-inch rounds. Place the rounds on a lined sheet tray and cook for 10 to 12 minutes, or until golden. Remove and let cool. Serve with Chocolate-Orange Mousse.

CHOCOLATE LAVA CAKE

8 OUNCES CHOCOLATE CHIPS
½ CUP HEAVY CREAM
1 CUP BUTTER
2 TEASPOONS CINNAMON
2 TEASPOONS SALT
4 EGGS
4 EGG YOLKS
1 CUP SUGAR
2 TEASPOONS VANILLA
½ CUP FLOUR
POWDERED SUGAR, FOR GARNISH

1. Preheat the oven to 400°F.
2. Using a double boiler (a metal bowl placed over a pot of simmering water), combine 4 ounces of chocolate chips with the cream, stirring occasionally until melted together. Transfer the chocolate to another container and refrigerate until firm to the touch. Reserve cold.
3. In a pan over low heat, melt together the remaining 4 ounces of chocolate chips with the butter, cinnamon, and salt until smooth and no chunks remain.
4. In the bowl of a stand mixer, whip together the eggs, egg yolks, sugar, and vanilla until the eggs have increased in volume and are light and fluffy (approximately 10 minutes). Fold the melted chocolate and butter into the whipped egg mixture, along with the flour, until just incorporated. Divide the batter in half.
5. Spray 6 oven-safe ramekins with nonstick spray. Portion one half of the batter into the ramekins. Using a disher or a scoop, divide the refrigerated chocolate and place 1 scoop in the center of each ramekin. Portion the remaining half of the batter into each dish, making sure to cover the chocolate centers.
6. Place the ramekins on a sheet tray and bake until the cakes are firm to the touch, approximately 20 minutes. Remove from the oven and let cool until warm. Sprinkle each cake with powdered sugar. Serve warm.

RED (OR BROWN) COWS

6 SCOOPS VANILLA ICE CREAM

3 CANS BIG RED (OR OTHER RED SODA OR ROOT BEER MADE WITH PURE CANE SUGAR)

1. Place one scoop of ice cream into each of 6 glasses.
2. Quickly pour ½ can soda over each scoop of ice cream until thick foam forms.
3. Serve immediately with a spoon.

GINGER PANNA COTTA WITH LEMON CURD AND COCONUT MACAROONS

Panna Cotta

⅓ CUP MILK
1 ENVELOPE POWDERED GELATIN
6 GINGER TEA BAGS OR SACHETS
2 ½ CUPS HEAVY CREAM
½ CUP SUGAR
1 TABLESPOON VANILLA
ZEST OF 2 LEMONS, FOR GARNISH

1. In a small bowl, mix together the milk and gelatin. Set aside and allow the gelatin to "bloom" (thicken the milk), approximately 10 minutes.
2. Place tea sachets in a small pot and tie or tape the strings to the handle. Add the cream, sugar, and vanilla to the pot and warm over medium to high heat. Ensure that the tea bags are deep enough in the cream so they will steep as it warms. Once the cream has heated to 190°F, stir in the milk mixture. Cook 2 additional minutes. Remove from the heat.
3. Spray 6 ramekins or similar containers with nonstick spray. Portion the warmed cream mixture into each of the ramekins. Allow to cool, uncovered, to room temperature. Then refrigerate until set, approximately 4 hours.

Lemon Curd

3 EGGS
1 CUP SUGAR
½ CUP LEMON JUICE
¼ CUP BUTTER, MELTED
ZEST OF 2 LEMONS

1. Using a double boiler (a metal bowl placed over a simmering pot of water), beat together the eggs and sugar until the mixture has turned a pale yellow and the graininess of the sugar dissipates (approximately 3 minutes). Stir in the lemon juice, butter, and lemon zest. Cook until the mixture has thickened, approximately 15 minutes, stirring frequently to avoid scrambling the eggs.
2. Remove the mixture from the bowl and chill 1 hour.

Coconut Macaroons

1 EGG WHITE
1 14-OUNCE PACKAGE SHREDDED COCONUT
ZEST OF 2 LEMONS
2 TEASPOONS GROUND GINGER
1 14-OUNCE CAN SWEETENED CONDENSED MILK

1. Preheat the oven to 325°F.
2. Whip the egg white until light and fluffy.
3. In a separate bowl, combine the coconut, lemon zest, ginger, and sweetened condensed milk. Fold in the whipped egg white.
4. Using a 1-ounce disher or large tablespoon, drop spoonfuls of the mixture onto a sheet tray with a silicone baking liner (or line the pan with a parchment sprayed with nonstick spray). Bake 17 minutes or until lightly browned around the edges.

Assembly

1. Using a tablespoon, place a spoonful of the chilled lemon curd onto the center of a plate. Use the back of the spoon to gently the spread the curd out into a circle.
2. The panna cotta is just barely set and requires delicate handling. Trace the inside perimeter of the ramekin with just the tip of a paring knife to release the panna cotta. Turn ramekin upside down and allow the panna cotta to fall into the palm of your hand. Gently place the panna cotta, still upside down, into the center of the lemon curd.
3. Place a macaroon on the side of each panna cotta and sprinkle with lemon zest before serving.

FLAN

1 CUP SUGAR
1 14-OUNCE CAN SWEETENED CONDENSED MILK
3 CUPS HEAVY CREAM
1 CUP WHOLE MILK
6 EGGS
2 TEASPOONS ALMOND EXTRACT
1 TEASPOON VANILLA EXTRACT
1 TEASPOON CINNAMON
ZEST OF 2 LEMONS

1. Preheat the oven to 350°F.
2. In a pan over medium heat, cook the sugar until it reaches a light brown caramel. Do not stir while cooking, but rather swirl the pot until the sugar is completely cooked and no lumps remain. Immediately distribute the cooked sugar in an even layer into 8 individual ramekins. (This step must be done immediately to avoid the sugar hardening too soon.) Set aside.
3. In a bowl, using a hand mixer or a stand mixer, beat together the remaining ingredients until smooth. Spray the hardened sugar ramekins with nonstick spray. Distribute the cream mixture evenly into the ramekins.
4. Place the ramekins into a 2-inch deep baking pan or dish. Gently pour hot tap water into the pan until the ramekins are ¾ submerged, taking care not to pour water into the ramekins themselves.
5. Carefully place the pan in the preheated oven without spilling water into the ramekins. Bake 45 to 50 minutes or until the custards are set. Remove pan from the oven and let the custards cool to room temperature. Once cooled, remove the ramekins from the pan and refrigerate 1 hour.
6. Gently run a knife around the exterior of the chilled flan (the knife should remain firmly against the edge of the ramekin, so as not to cut the flan). Place a small plate on top of the ramekin, serving side toward the flan. Turn over and allow the flan to fall onto the plate. Serve chilled.

ICE CREAM SANDWICHES

½ CUP SUGAR
½ CUP BROWN SUGAR
½ CUP AGAVE NECTAR
1 CUP BUTTER, SOFTENED
2 EGGS
2 ¼ CUPS FLOUR
½ TEASPOON BAKING POWDER
2 TEASPOONS CINNAMON
2 TEASPOONS GROUND GINGER
1 TEASPOON SALT
1 TABLESPOON VANILLA
1 CUP MILK CHOCOLATE CHIPS
1 CUP DARK CHOCOLATE CHIPS
VANILLA ICE CREAM

1. Preheat the oven to 375°F.
2. In the bowl of a stand mixer, cream together the sugar, brown sugar, agave nectar, and butter until fluffy. Mix in the eggs until fully incorporated.
3. Stir in the flour, baking powder, cinnamon, ginger, salt, and vanilla. Once incorporated, stir in the chocolate chips.
4. Using a 2-ounce scoop or tablespoon, form the dough into balls and drop onto unlined, unsprayed sheet trays, no more than 12 to a pan. Bake for 12 minutes.
5. Remove the cookies from the oven and let cool to room temperature. Arrange all the cookies in a single layer on a sheet tray and place in the freezer for 30 minutes.
6. Remove the cookies from the freezer. Place one large scoop of ice cream on the bottom of one cookie. Place another cookie on top of the ice cream. Gently squeeze the cookies together until the ice cream has reached the edges. Serve immediately or store in the freezer (sandwiches should be thawed at least 5 minutes before serving).

MOLTEN HOT CHOCOLATE AND MARSHMALLOWS

Hot Chocolate

3 QUARTS WHOLE MILK
1 QUART HEAVY CREAM
¼ CUP COCOA POWDER
2 TABLESPOONS CINNAMON
¼ CUP VANILLA
4 CUPS CHOCOLATE CHIPS

1. In a saucepan over medium to high heat, warm the milk, cream, cocoa powder, cinnamon, and vanilla, stirring often to avoid charring. Do not allow the mixture to boil.
2. Once the mixture is simmering, stir in the chocolate chips until completely melted, stirring frequently. Cook over medium heat for 10 minutes.
3. Serve hot, with Marshmallows (recipe follows).

Marshmallows

A stand mixer is required for this recipe due to the high speed needed to whip the marshmallows.

3 ENVELOPES POWDERED GELATIN
½ CUP PLUS ½ CUP COLD WATER
1 ½ CUPS SUGAR
1 CUP CORN SYRUP
1 TABLESPOON VANILLA
2 CUPS POWDERED SUGAR (APPROXIMATE)

1. In the bowl of a stand mixer, combine the gelatin with ½ cup of cold water and allow the gelatin to "bloom" into a light gel.
2. In a small pan, combine the remaining water, sugar, and corn syrup. Whisk together to incorporate the sugar. Cook over high heat until the mixture reaches 240°F. Remove from heat and pour over the bloomed gelatin. Add the vanilla.

3. Using the mixer's whisk attachment (or a whip), beat the sugar and gelatin for approximately 15 minutes, or until the mixture has quadrupled in volume and has cooled enough to touch the bowl without getting burned.
4. While the sugar and gelatin are whipping, generously spray a 9 × 13-inch baking pan or dish with nonstick spray. Place ¼ cup of powdered sugar in the pan and turn the pan to coat all sides.
5. Once the sugar mixture is ready, pour immediately into the dusted pan. Tap the pan against a hard surface to even out the mixture. Gently dust the top with enough powdered sugar to lightly cover (it shouldn't feel sticky). Allow to set 4 hours.
6. Turn the pan over onto a cutting board dusted with powdered sugar. Cut the sheet into 1-inch squares. Toss the cut marshmallows in a bowl with the powdered sugar. Store covered in powdered sugar to prevent sticking.

CREPES WITH STRAWBERRY JAM AND WHIPPED CREAM

Crepes

1 ¼ CUPS FLOUR
2 TABLESPOONS SUGAR
½ TEASPOON SALT
3 EGGS
2 CUPS WHOLE MILK
1 TABLESPOON VANILLA
2 TABLESPOONS BUTTER, MELTED
1 CUP HEAVY CREAM
1 TEASPOON SUGAR

1. In a bowl, mix together the flour, sugar, salt, eggs, milk, and vanilla using a whisk, a hand mixer, or the whip attachment of a stand mixer. Add the butter until fully incorporated.
2. Pass the batter through a mesh strainer into a bowl, whisking the sides of the strainer to work out any lumps in the batter.
3. Spray a nonstick pan with cooking spray. Warm the pan over medium-high heat until a hand held over the surface feels hot. Using a ladle or a measuring cup, pour enough batter into the pan to coat the bottom with a thin layer. Let cook approximately 1 minute, or until the visible side of the crepe looks just barely cooked. Flip very gently in the pan (or use a spatula if necessary). Cook the remaining side for 30 seconds.
4. Remove each crepe from the pan and let cool 5 minutes. Fold each crepe in half, then in half again.
5. In a bowl, whisk together the cream and sugar until light peaks have formed and the cream is still slightly runny. Serve over warm crepes topped with Strawberry Jam (recipe follows).

Strawberry Jam

2 CUPS STRAWBERRIES, CHOPPED
1 CUP BROWN SUGAR, LIGHTLY PACKED
½ CUP LEMON JUICE
1 TEASPOON SALT

1. Place all ingredients in a small saucepan. Bring the mixture to a boil over high heat, then reduce to a simmer.
2. Let simmer until the mixture reaches a syrup-like consistency, approximately 25 minutes. Serve warm over warm crepes.

CHOCOLATE CHIP FRITTERS

2 CUPS FLOUR
2 TEASPOONS BAKING POWDER
¼ CUP SUGAR
1 TEASPOON SALT
2 EGGS
1 CUP WHOLE MILK
2 TABLESPOONS BUTTER, MELTED
2 CUPS DARK CHOCOLATE CHIPS
2 QUARTS OIL, FOR FRYING
VANILLA ICE CREAM, FOR SERVING

1. In a small pot, heat the oil to 365°F. In a bowl, combine the flour, baking powder, sugar, and salt. Set aside.
2. In a bowl, beat together the eggs, milk, and butter. Combine the flour and the egg mixtures until a thick, smooth batter is formed. Fold in the chocolate chips.
3. Drop tablespoons of the batter into the hot oil. Fry until golden brown. Remove from the oil and let drain on a wire rack. Serve warm with ice cream.

APPLE COBBLER WITH VANILLA ICE CREAM

4 LARGE APPLES
1 CUP BROWN SUGAR
⅓ CUP LEMON JUICE
2 CUPS FLOUR
2 TEASPOONS BAKING POWDER
1 TEASPOON SALT
1 TEASPOON GROUND GINGER
1 TEASPOON GROUND CLOVES
2 TEASPOONS CINNAMON
2 EGGS
1 ½ CUPS SUGAR
½ CUP WHOLE MILK
4 TABLESPOONS BUTTER, MELTED

1. Preheat the oven to 350°F.
2. Thinly slice each apple and place in a bowl with the brown sugar and lemon juice. Toss together until the apples are evenly coated. Spray a 9 × 13-inch baking dish with nonstick spray. Place the glazed apples in the dish in an even layer.
3. Sift together the flour, baking powder, salt, ginger, cloves, and cinnamon.
4. In a bowl, beat together the eggs, sugar, and milk using a whisk or the whip attachment of a stand mixer. Add the flour mixture and stir until batter becomes thick. Add the butter, and beat on low until the batter has loosened up.
5. Pour the batter over the apples in the baking dish. Spread evenly with a spatula.
6. Bake for 30 to 33 minutes, or until a knife inserted comes out free of batter (there may be some glaze on the knife from the apples). Let cool until warm, approximately 20 minutes.
7. Serve with vanilla ice cream or whipped cream.

BREAKFAST AND BRUNCH

Brunch, always served buffet style, is the one meal that has remained relatively unchanged over the course of Temple Ranch's history. Although it is the only moment throughout any weekend when history outweighs creativity in the kitchen, brunch at Temple Ranch extends beyond Texas classics and creates its own tradition. Combining regional cuisine, Mexican influence, and country cooking, brunch remains the most important meal held at the ranch. Fried quail recalls the earlier months in the hunting season before deer were the only thing on everyone's mind. Venison in its various preparations reminds hunters of their time spent hunkered down in the blinds.

During brunch, guests recall the weekend's events and talk about the coming week. If they don't frequent the ranch regularly, brunch may be a chance to say a leisurely goodbye and make plans for when they might next return. But without fail, at the end of every brunch, guests in attendance, from young hunters to old friends, are asked outside to pose for a group photograph—one more memory to catalog as part of the ranch's long history.

In deciding where to put the brunch recipes within the book, it seemed only appropriate to put them at the end. To me, brunch has always been about decadence—the simple luxury of having enough time to enjoy a long, relaxing meal to mark the week's true end. It is also the meal that people seem to savor the most, eat at the slowest pace. Week in and week out, while working at the Temple Ranch, I felt I was giving each guest the gift of leisure. Really, what more can a chef ask for?

MIGAS

There isn't one correct recipe for migas, but any Tex-Mex migas recipe will always include tortillas and eggs. Migas are very much like tacos in that there are countless variations and everyone has their favorite. After eating far too many of these variations, though, I've come to a decision as to how they should be represented, and I'm fairly confident that it's hard to get much better migas than those detailed below. This recipe does take more time and requires additional steps, but the use of freshly fried tortillas makes for a flavor that is second to none. The nuttiness of the oil lingers on the strips and makes the dish taste like a breakfast burrito turned inside out. Simply delicious!

OIL, FOR FRYING
12 CORN TORTILLAS
2 TABLESPOONS CANOLA OIL
1 JALAPEÑO, SEEDED AND DICED
½ ONION, DICED
1 RED BELL PEPPER, DICED
12 EGGS
1 CUP WHOLE MILK
SALT AND BLACK PEPPER, TO TASTE
1 CUP AMERICAN CHEESE, SHREDDED

1. Divide the tortillas in half. Cut 6 into 1-inch strips, and cut 6 into ⅛-inch strips. Fry separately until golden brown. Set aside.
2. In a nonstick sauté pan, warm the canola oil over medium-high heat until it flows freely. Add the jalapeño, onion, and bell pepper. Sauté 1 minute. Add the thick tortilla strips.
3. In a bowl, combine the eggs, milk, salt, and pepper. Whisk together until all yolks are fully incorporated.
4. Pour eggs over vegetable mixture in the pan and reduce heat to medium. Cook until eggs are fluffy and no moisture remains in the pan, approximately 10 minutes. Remove from heat. Top with cheese and crispy, thin tortilla strips. Serve in a bowl, family style.

FRIED QUAIL

8 QUAIL, WHOLE
2 CUPS BUTTERMILK
2 TABLESPOONS BLACK PEPPERCORNS
1 TABLESPOON CUMIN
1 TABLESPOON DRIED SAGE
1 TABLESPOON PLUS 1 TABLESPOON SALT
1 BAY LEAF
2 CUPS FLOUR
1 TABLESPOON BLACK PEPPER
CANOLA OIL, FOR FRYING

1. Marinate the quail overnight in the buttermilk, peppercorns, cumin, sage, 1 tablespoon salt, and bay leaf.
2. In a bowl, mix flour with the pepper and remaining 1 tablespoon salt. Remove the quail from the marinade and dredge heavily in seasoned flour.
3. Heat canola oil to 375°F. Deep-fry quail until golden brown. Serve as part of a buffet or alongside Biscuits and Gravy (see recipe on p. 196).

CHILAQUILES

OIL, FOR FRYING
15 CORN TORTILLAS
1 28-OUNCE CAN WHOLE PEELED TOMATOES
3 TABLESPOONS CANOLA OIL
1 ONION, DICED
4 ANCHO CHILES, STEMMED AND SEEDED
2 CLOVES GARLIC, MINCED
2 TABLESPOONS SALT
1 TABLESPOON BLACK PEPPER
2 TABLESPOONS CHILI POWDER
1 BUNCH CILANTRO, CHOPPED
EGGS (1 PER SERVING)
SHREDDED PEPPER JACK CHEESE, FOR GARNISH

1. Preheat the oven to 400°F.
2. In a deep fryer or a pot, heat the oil to 365°F. Cut each tortilla into 1-inch strips. Deep-fry in the hot oil until crisp. Remove strips and let drain on a wire rack. Set aside.
3. Using a food processor, puree the tomatoes and their juice until smooth. Set aside.
4. In a sauté pan, warm the canola oil over high heat until it flows freely. Add the onion and ancho chiles to the pan. Sauté until the onions are transparent, approximately 3 minutes. Add the garlic and sauté an additional 2 minutes, or until the aroma of the garlic and chile is strong.
5. Add the salt, pepper, and chili powder to the pan. Sauté 1 minute. Add the pureed tomatoes and bring to a boil, then reduce to a simmer. Let cook 10 minutes.
6. Remove the pan from the heat. Stir in the cilantro. Divide into two batches and puree each in a food processor until nearly smooth (small chunks of the anchos may still be visible).
7. In a large mixing bowl, toss the fried tortilla strips in the warm salsa until generously coated. Place the coated strips in a Pyrex or other oven-safe dish that can double as a serving dish. Place the dish in the oven and cook approximately 15 minutes, until the salsa has lost its sheen and the tortilla strips begin to char lightly. Set aside any leftover salsa, to be served alongside the chilaquiles.
8. While the tortillas are baking, fry at least one egg for each serving. Remove baked strips from the oven and top with the fried eggs. Garnish with cheese and serve hot.

BISCUITS AND GRAVY

Biscuits

½ CUP BUTTER
2 CUPS FLOUR, PLUS ADDITIONAL FOR FOLDING DOUGH
4 TEASPOONS BAKING POWDER
¾ CUP BUTTERMILK
1 EGG
2 TEASPOONS SUGAR
1 TABLESPOON SALT
1 TEASPOON BLACK PEPPER

1. Preheat the oven to 425°F.
2. Dice the butter into small chunks. Add the flour and knead the butter into it until small pellets form.
3. In the bowl of a stand mixer (or by hand, if necessary), combine the flour mixture with the baking powder, buttermilk, egg, sugar, salt, and pepper. Beat with the paddle attachment until all ingredients are just blended.
4. Remove the dough from the bowl, making sure to scrape the sides and paddle for all remnants. Place dough on a lightly floured surface and roll in flour until a dusted ball forms. Flatten the ball and begin folding the dough in half from side to side, slightly flattening the dough after each fold to ensure flakiness in the biscuits. Repeat 20 times.
5. Once the folding is completed, use a lightly floured rolling pin to roll out the dough into a sheet roughly ¾ inch thick. Using a ring mold or a biscuit cutter, cut out biscuits to desired size. (Be sure not to turn the mold when you push through the dough. This will seal the edges and create a less fluffy biscuit.)
6. Bake for 11 minutes. Serve warm with Sausage Gravy (recipe follows).

Sausage Gravy

1 CUP BUTTER
1 CUP FLOUR
1 QUART HEAVY CREAM (OR WHOLE MILK, REDUCED-FAT MILK, OR SOME COMBINATION OF THE THREE)
1 QUART BUTTERMILK
2 TABLESPOONS SALT
1 TABLESPOON BLACK PEPPER
1 POUND GROUND PORK
1 TABLESPOON GROUND SAGE

1. Using a thick-bottomed pot or saucepan, warm the butter until it has just melted. Add the flour and cook on medium to high heat for 4 minutes, stirring frequently.
2. Once the mixture has started to change colors and develops a slightly nutty aroma, add the milk, buttermilk, salt, and pepper. Whisk together. Cook over medium heat until the mixture starts to thicken to desired consistency, approximately 10 minutes (varies depending on the cream or milk used). If the gravy becomes too thick, add more cream or water to thin out.
3. In a separate pan, cook the ground pork with the sage over medium-high heat until cooked through.
4. Combine the pork with the gravy. Serve warm over biscuits.

SPANISH-STYLE "TORTILLA" WITH CREAM SAUCE

Known to Italians as a *frittata*, this dish is not only served for breakfast. Various combinations of vegetables and meats can be added for different preparations. The tortilla can be served warm, at room temperature, or cold. For breakfast, it provides a hearty, protein packed start to the day. As a dinner dish, it can be cooked ahead of time and then cubed for appetizers. Be sure to use only heavy cream, however, as it provides the airy "soufflé" action on which the tortilla depends.

Tortilla

2 TABLESPOONS OLIVE OIL
12 EGGS
1 CUP HEAVY CREAM
1 TEASPOON PAPRIKA
4 TEASPOONS SALT
2 TEASPOONS BLACK PEPPER
½ ONION, JULIENNED
1 RUSSET POTATO
1 CUP SPINACH

1. Preheated oven to 350°F.
2. In a 12-inch cast iron pan, warm the oil until it flows freely. Tilt the pan so the oil coats all sides up to the rim.
3. In a medium-size bowl, beat together the eggs, cream, paprika, salt, and pepper.
4. Sauté the onion and potato in the hot oil for 1 minute. Stir in the spinach.
5. Without moving the pan, pour the egg mixture over the vegetables before the spinach completely wilts. Remove pan from heat.
6. Bake for 30 minutes, or until a knife inserted comes out clean. Let rest 10 minutes in the pan.
7. For immediate serving, flip the pan over onto a cutting board. The tortilla should release freely. Cut into triangular slices and serve with Cream Sauce (recipe follows).

Cream Sauce

2 CUPS SOUR CREAM
6 TABLESPOONS LEMON JUICE
3 TABLESPOONS DIJON MUSTARD
1 TEASPOON PAPRIKA
2 TABLESPOONS SALT
1 TEASPOON BLACK PEPPER

1. Mix all ingredients together in a bowl until incorporated.
2. Serve over warm tortilla.

BLACK-EYED PEAS

This dish is typically served for New Year's Day brunch.

6 TABLESPOONS CANOLA OIL
1 ONION, DICED
2 TABLESPOONS SALT
1 TABLESPOON BLACK PEPPER
1 TABLESPOON CHILI POWDER
2 CLOVES GARLIC, MINCED
4 CUPS BLACK-EYED PEAS, FRESH
4 CUPS WATER
½ CUP BUTTER

1. In a 6-quart saucepan or similar, warm the canola oil over medium heat until it flows freely. Sauté the onion with the salt, pepper, and chili powder until translucent, approximately 2 minutes. Add the garlic and then the black-eyed peas. Sauté until all ingredients have been glazed with the oil.
2. Pour in the water. Bring to a boil, then reduce to a simmer.
3. Once the beans have cooked through but still have bite, approximately 20 minutes, add the butter. Cook 5 more minutes. Serve warm.

BAKED EGGS AND TOMATO

1 28-OUNCE CAN WHOLE PEELED TOMATOES, INCLUDING JUICE
1 6-OUNCE CAN TOMATO PASTE
1 BUNCH PARSLEY, CHOPPED (FOR TOMATO SAUCE AND GARNISH)
½ CUP PLUS ½ CUP OLIVE OIL
2 TABLESPOONS SALT
2 TEASPOONS PEPPER
8 EGGS
CRÈME FRAÎCHE OR GREEK YOGURT
1 BUNCH PARSLEY, CHOPPED (FOR GARNISH)
PITA BREAD

1. Preheat the oven to 375°F.
2. Using a food processor, puree the tomatoes, tomato paste, parsley, ½ cup olive oil, salt, and pepper until smooth.
3. Heat tomato mixture in a pan until just boiling. Remove from heat and cool.
4. Cover the bottom of 4 oven-safe casserole dishes with half of tomato sauce. Crack 2 eggs on top of each dish of tomato sauce. Lightly cover the eggs with the remaining sauce so that the yolks are visible and the whites are just covered.
5. Drizzle the remaining ½ cup olive oil over the yolks. (This will help prevent the yolks from cooking before the whites.) Bake until the whites are just visibly set, approximately 15 minutes.
6. Remove from oven. Garnish each dish with a spoonful of yogurt and parsley. Serve warm with pita bread.

EGGS BENEDICT

If you were to ask Buddy Temple his thoughts on breakfast, he would most likely tell you two things. First, he would say that migas are his favorite dish. Second, and more important, he would tell you that he considers himself to be an expert on the art form that is Eggs Benedict. Get them right, and he will praise the ground you cook on. Get them wrong, and you will be told immediately what mistakes you made (constructively, of course!).

The key is serving a classic English muffin that isn't too thick and has been toasted until crisp. The eggs must be strained to remove all the poaching liquid so it doesn't water down the hollandaise. Finally, the ham or Canadian bacon must be cooked long enough that it isn't dried out but still has a visible char for that added flavor kick. When you are serving multiple people at once, timing this whole process can be a nightmare. If you are successful, though, the result is easily the most revered breakfast classic of all time.

Admittedly, I have made plenty of mistakes with Eggs Benedict, from not straining enough of the poaching water to serving too thick of an artisan English muffin. By now, however, I have managed to get them just right. And if you are as avid a lover of Eggs Benedict as Buddy Temple is, you'll know exactly what that means.

Hollandaise

2 CUPS BUTTER
2 EGGS
1 TABLESPOON LEMON JUICE
1 TABLESPOON SALT
1 TEASPOON BLACK PEPPER
1 TEASPOON PAPRIKA

1. In a pan, melt the butter over low to medium heat. Set aside.
2. Crack the eggs into the bowl of a food processor. Add the lemon juice, salt, pepper, and paprika. Blend until smooth. Leave the machine running.
3. Immediately begin to pour the butter slowly into the food processor. The result should be a viscous, creamy sauce.
4. Pour the sauce into a thick ceramic bowl or carafe. Place into a warm water bath until ready to serve.

Assembly

2 QUARTS WATER
1 CUP WHITE VINEGAR
1 TABLESPOON SALT
4 PIECES HAM OR CANADIAN BACON
4 EGGS
2 ENGLISH MUFFINS

1. In a 4- or 6-quart saucepan, bring the water, vinegar, and salt to a boil. Once boiling, reduce to a low simmer.
2. In a sauté pan over medium to high heat, cook the ham for 3 minutes on each side or until lightly charred.
3. To poach eggs, use a spoon to gently create a whirlpool in the simmering water. Crack 1 egg into the spinning water. Repeat for the remaining eggs.
4. Toast the muffins until golden brown. Remove from the toaster and place a piece of cooked ham on top of each muffin half.
5. Once the egg whites gently spring back when touched (approximately 6 minutes), remove the poached eggs from the water with a slotted spoon, taking care to strain off as much water as possible. Place one egg on top of each muffin half.
6. Glaze each egg with a ladleful of hollandaise. Serve warm.

HASH BROWN CAKES

8 RUSSET POTATOES
2 TABLESPOONS PAPRIKA
1 TABLESPOON CHILI POWDER
4 TABLESPOONS SALT
1 TABLESPOON BLACK PEPPER
OIL, FOR FRYING

1. Preheat the oven to 375°F. Line a sheet tray with parchment paper and spray generously with nonstick cooking spray.
2. Using either a box grater or the shredder attachment of a food processor, shred the potatoes. In a bowl, mix potatoes with spices, salt, and pepper.
3. Using both hands, grab portions of the seasoned potatoes and squeeze out excess liquid. Place each squeezed portion onto the sprayed sheet tray in level clumps. Repeat until the sheet tray is packed tightly with large potato clumps. Then pat the clumps down by hand so they are flush to the rim of the tray.
4. Spray another sheet of parchment with nonstick spray. Place the sprayed side on top of the flattened potatoes. Bake for 1 hour. Remove from oven and let cool overnight.
5. Remove the top sheet of parchment from the potatoes. Cut the cooked cake to desired portion size. Rectangles, squares, or triangles make the best presentation.
6. Deep-fry potato cakes approximately 3 minutes or until golden brown. Serve warm.

FRUIT SALAD

1 CUP KIWI, PEELED AND QUARTERED
1 CUP BANANAS, SLICED
1 CUP BLUEBERRIES
1 CUP STRAWBERRIES, STEMMED AND QUARTERED
½ CUP LIGHT AGAVE NECTAR
MINT OR CILANTRO, FOR GARNISH (OPTIONAL)

1. Combine the fruits in a bowl.
2. Pour the agave nectar over the fruit and toss gently until all fruits are covered.
3. Serve chilled. For an extra elegant touch to a breakfast buffet, garnish with chopped herbs such as mint or cilantro.

CONDIMENTS, DRESSINGS, GARNISHES, AND MARINADES

BRINE

This brine works well for venison, pork, and even chicken.

4 QUARTS WARM WATER
2 CLOVES GARLIC
1 TABLESPOON CLOVES, WHOLE
1 BAY LEAF
2 TABLESPOONS BLACK PEPPERCORNS
1 TABLESPOON FENNEL SEED
1 TABLESPOON SALT
1 LEMON, HALVED

1. Combine all ingredients, ensuring salt has dissolved.

GUACAMOLE

2 RIPE HASS AVOCADOS
1 JALAPEÑO, SEEDED AND DICED
1 ROMA TOMATO, DICED
½ ONION, DICED
¼ CUP CILANTRO, CHOPPED
2 TABLESPOONS LIME JUICE
1 TABLESPOON SALT
1 TEASPOON BLACK PEPPER

1. Cut the avocados in half and remove the pits. Scrape the flesh into a bowl.
2. Add the jalapeño, tomato, onion, cilantro, lime juice, salt, and pepper. Using your hands, mash the avocado with the other ingredients until a thick paste has formed.
3. Serve slightly chilled with such dishes as Mary Cadena's Enchiladas (see recipe on p. 76), Chicken Fajitas (p. 85), or Chiles Rellenos (p. 142).

PICKLED MUSTARD SEEDS

1 CUP WHOLE MUSTARD SEEDS
1 ½ CUPS SHERRY VINEGAR
½ CUP APPLE CIDER VINEGAR
1 CUP SUGAR
¼ CUP SALT
1 TABLESPOON CORIANDER SEED
2 TABLESPOONS BLACK PEPPERCORNS
2 BAY LEAVES

1. Place the mustard seeds in a 1-quart container that has a lid.
2. In a saucepan, combine all other ingredients. Bring to a boil over high heat and let cook 2 minutes, until sugar has completely dissolved. Remove the pickling juice from the heat and strain over the mustard seeds.
3. Let sit 2 days before serving.

PICKLED RED ONIONS

3 RED ONIONS
1 ½ CUPS APPLE CIDER VINEGAR
½ CUP CHAMPAGNE VINEGAR
1 CUP SUGAR
⅓ CUP SALT
2 TABLESPOONS CORIANDER SEED
2 TABLESPOONS BLACK PEPPERCORNS
2 BAY LEAVES

1. Using a mandoline slicer, thinly slice each onion. Place the sliced onions in a 4-quart (or larger) container.
2. In a saucepan, combine all other ingredients. Bring to a boil over high heat and let cook 2 minutes, until sugar has completely dissolved. Remove the pickling juice from the heat and strain over the sliced onions.
3. Place two plates or a similarly heavy object on top of the onions to keep them in the pickling juice. Let sit 2 days before serving. Serve with such dishes as Chicken Fajitas (see recipe on p. 85), Boggy Slough Chili (p. 93), Venison Chili (p. 90), Green Pozole (p. 95), or any type of barbecue.

CIDER-VANILLA VINAIGRETTE

¼ CUP APPLE CIDER VINEGAR
1 TABLESPOON DIJON MUSTARD
1 TABLESPOON AGAVE NECTAR
1 TEASPOON VANILLA EXTRACT
2 TEASPOONS SALT
1 TEASPOON BLACK PEPPER
1 CUP CANOLA OIL

1. Place a mixing bowl on a wet towel to prevent the bowl from spinning. Whisk together the vinegar, mustard, agave nectar, vanilla, salt, and pepper until fully incorporated.
2. Slowly drizzle in the oil while whisking quickly to form a thick, glossy dressing. Serve over Green Salad (see recipe on p. 56) or any other salad.

FRESH AIOLI

Will make slightly more than two cups

2 EGGS
1 CLOVE GARLIC
½ CUP LEMON JUICE
2 TEASPOONS SALT
1 TEASPOON BLACK PEPPER
2 CUPS CANOLA OIL

1. In the bowl of a food processor, combine the eggs, garlic, lemon juice, salt, and pepper. Grind until smooth.
2. With the egg mixture spinning, slowly pour in the oil in a steady stream until all is fully incorporated. Serve cold with fish, quail, or mushroom dishes, or use as a base in other recipes such as potato salad or chicken salad.

TEMPLE FAMILY MAYONNAISE

1 EGG
1 ¾ CUP LIGHT OLIVE OIL
JUICE OF 1 LEMON
1 TEASPOON SALT
1 TEASPOON PAPRIKA (SUBSTITUTE OTHER FLAVORINGS, SUCH AS DILL OR GARLIC, FOR OTHER MAYONNAISES)

1. Using a food processor or a whisk, beat one egg. Slowly add oil in a thin stream to emulsify. If mayonnaise curdles (usually when oil is added too rapidly), beat egg in a separate bowl, then slowly add curdled mayonnaise to emulsify.
2. Add lemon juice, salt, and paprika until well mixed. Serve with burgers, sandwiches, etc.

SCRATCH TARTAR SAUCE

2 CUPS FRESH AIOLI (SEE RECIPE ON P. 215)
½ CUP PICKLED RED ONIONS (SEE RECIPE ON P. 214), ROUGHLY CHOPPED
½ CUP CAPERS
2 TABLESPOONS PARSLEY, FINELY CHOPPED
2 TEASPOONS BLACK PEPPER

1. In a bowl, whisk together all ingredients.
2. Serve chilled with Robalo-Style Snapper (see recipe on p. 68), Fried Fish and Dirty Rice (p. 128), and other fish dishes.

ALLEN JONAS'S TARTAR SAUCE

½ CUP MAYONNAISE
⅔ CUP DILL PICKLE RELISH, JUICE DRAINED AND SET ASIDE
2 TABLESPOONS ONION, MINCED
1 TABLESPOON LEMON JUICE

1. In a bowl, whisk together all ingredients.
2. Add juice from the relish to thin sauce to desired consistency.
3. Serve chilled.

RANCH DRESSING

2 CUPS MAYONNAISE
2 ½ CUPS BUTTERMILK
2 TABLESPOONS DRIED PARSLEY
1 TABLESPOON BLACK PEPPER
5 TEASPOONS SALT

1. In a bowl, whisk together the mayonnaise and buttermilk until evenly combined. Add the parsley, pepper, and salt. Mix together well.
2. Serve chilled with Iceberg Wedge (see recipe on p. 59) or as a complement to pizza.

BREAD CRUMBS

1 BAGUETTE
½ CUP CANOLA OIL
1 TABLESPOON SALT
1 TEASPOON BLACK PEPPER

1. Preheat the oven to 375°F.
2. Cut the baguette into large chunks. In a bowl, toss the chopped baguette with the oil, salt, and pepper until all chunks are evenly coated. Roast until golden brown, approximately 20 minutes. Remove from oven and let cool to room temperature.
3. Once bread is cool, place in the bowl of a food processor and grind until coarse crumbs are formed. Use to garnish salads, appetizers, and other meals.

ACKNOWLEDGMENTS

We are grateful, always, to our manager, Robert Sanders; our facilities and events manager, Jenny Sanders; our ranch mascot, Nate Sanders; our assistant manager, Kevin Anderson; our wrangler, Joe Fox; our hospitality team, Mary Cadena, Amyle Ridgeway, and Connie Ramos; and all the others who work so hard to make the ranch a special place to be. And we have grateful hearts for all the folks who came before them, especially David and Juanita Smith. Special thanks to Archeological Consultants, Inc., whose research grounds our history in facts, for their diligent work on our historical gems: Jim Warren (owner/operator), Art Romine, and Bobby Jemmison, with additional assistance from T.E. and Colton Warren, Sonny Whitley, Wayne Wernli, and Rindle Wilson. We appreciate the excellent article by Mike Cox, "Reviving the Ranch," published in *Texas Parks and Wildlife* magazine. Finally, we are grateful to Maureen Hafernik, our business assistant, who keeps us all on track.

Our daughter, Susie Temple, expresses the gratitude that our whole family feels: "I think one of the special things about meals at the ranch—particularly lunch—is sitting down with the people who actually *work* the ranch. It's not only a time to visit with family and friends but also a time to be immersed in the daily life of the ranch—an authentic day—where you can learn about anything from tracking turkeys and scoring big bucks, to horse training and quail numbers, to the drought and habitat restoration. It's a time to connect with Robert, Jenny, Joe, or Kevin and make a plan for your afternoon activity—be it deer hunting, quail hunting, or swimming. It's about the people who work there and their dedication to our vision that make the ranch special."

Buddy and I thank Patrick for all the work that he put into compiling this beautiful book for us. We dedicate the *Temple Ranch Cookbook* to our talented staff, to our family, friends, and guests over the years, and to our children and their spouses, Whitney Temple, John Hurst, Hannah Temple and Christopher Sanders, Susie Temple and Rob Feagin, and our adorable grandchildren, Lilly, Maggie, Walter, Mary Ellen, Robert, and Helen.

– ELLEN TEMPLE

I would like to thank the Temple family for giving me the chance to cook at the Temple Ranch. You have no idea how much this opportunity, your compliments, your encouragement, and your enthusiasm for eating have made a difference in my life. I am forever grateful.

I would also like to thank:

The Sanders family for their hospitality and for always making sure that I had the tools to do my best.

David Nix for capturing so perfectly with his lens the labor of love that so many cooks have put forth in the last twenty years.

Mary for laughing. A lot. Always.

Connie, Josie, Vicki, and Bill for their unconditional help.

Kevin for his perpetual good mood.

Rene, Laura, Richard, Dean, Jason, Andrew, Shawn, Ned, and the countless other chefs who have made my time spent cooking in Texas nothing short of perfect. This book would not have happened without each and every one of you.

I would especially like to thank my wife, Doris, for guiding me through—with so much patience.

–PATRICK HIEGER

INDEX

NOTE: Page numbers in *italics* indicate a photograph.

T

V

W